GETTING PAST
YOUR PAST

GETTING PAST YOUR PAST

FINDING FREEDOM FROM THE PAIN OF REGRET

SUSAN WILKINSON

Multnomah Publishers® *Sisters, Oregon*

GETTING PAST YOUR PAST
published by Multnomah Publishers, Inc.

© 2000 by Susan Wilkinson
International Standard Book Number: 1-57673-739-X

Cover image by Tamara Reynolds Photography
Cover design by Uttley/DouPonce DesignWorks

Scripture quotations are from:
The Holy Bible, New International Version
© 1973, 1984 by International Bible Society,
used by permission of Zondervan Publishing House

Also quoted:
New American Standard Bible (NASB)
© 1960, 1977 by the Lockman Foundation

The Holy Bible, King James Version (KJV)

The Holy Bible Revised Standard Version Bible (RSV)
© 1946, 1952 by the Division of Christian Education
of the National Council of the Churches of Christ
in the United States of America

New Revised Standard Version Bible (NRSV)
© 1989 by the Division of Christian Education
of the National Council of Churches of Christ
in the United States of America

The New Testament in Modern English, Revised Edition (PHP)
© 1958, 1960, 1972 by J. B. Phillips

Some details in this book (including names of people, cities, and job titles) have been changed.

Multnomah is a trademark of Multnomah Publishers, Inc.,
and is registered in the U.S. Patent and Trademark Office.
The colophon is a trademark of Multnomah Publishers, Inc.

Printed in the United States of America

For information:
MULTNOMAH PUBLISHERS, INC. • P.O. BOX 1720 • SISTERS, OREGON 97759

Library of Congress Cataloging-in-Publication Data:

Wilkinson, Susan.
    Getting past your past: finding freedom from the pain of regret / Susan Wilkinson.
       p. cm.
    ISBN 1-57673-739-X (pbk.)
    1. Regret—Religious aspects—Christianity. I. Title
    BV4909.W54 2000
    248.8'6—dc21

                                00-010356

00 01 02 03 04 05 — 10 9 8 7 6 5 4 3 2 1 0

This book is dedicated to the fight for Joy.

Contents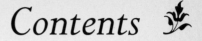

Acknowledgments

❧ THIS BOOK has been an immense joy to write. That is due in no small part to the following people. To each a heartfelt thank you....

Dad and Denise—for giving up your home for eight months (!), driving for the carpool, shopping for groceries, cleaning house, maintaining my car, and doing everything in between. Those things alone should qualify you for parents of the year, but there is so much more. You have both played a crucial part in many other areas of my life, especially in my spiritual growth. Dad, you remain my number one cheerleader—a vital role for any writer working in solitude. And Denise, were it not for your wisdom, vision, and willingness to be my sounding board, this book may not have been written.

Jeannie and Jeff—for your support, patience, carpooling, homework help, and meal preparation, all of which you did joyfully when we suddenly descended upon your life. Without you, this book would not have been completed on time.

Lindsey O'Connor—you know, there just aren't words, my friend. The Lord knows, and so do I, that if it weren't for your encouragement, wisdom, teaching, and willing spirit (not to mention your hidden marketing abilities!) it's likely that I would still be waiting to pursue my dream of writing. Thank *you* for being my mentor and cheerleader. I thank *God* that you are my kindred spirit.

Grammy and John—who would have thought that I would be thanking my grandparents for putting up with my parents for eight months? Thank you for opening your home to my parents so they could open their home to us. I love you both.

Pastor Jeff Moorehead and Mike and Margaret Hentschel—for analyzing my words and making me accountable for them. Your insight and knowledge have been invaluable to me. The time and wisdom you applied to these pages are evident in the final product.

Nancy Robertson—for taking care of my home in Texas for eight months, but mostly for loving my children and me. You have the most loving servant's heart I've ever had the privilege to know. Having you in my life makes me much richer.

Pam Ahern—for dotting my i's and crossing my t's, for struggling to get computer literate just for me, and for taking care of me and loving me when I needed it most.

Kerry Parker—for being my computer guru (you are the king, baby!) and for keeping me company through long hours of writing and struggling.

Gerard Smith—for knowing exactly what to say and when to say it. Your belief that I have something to say and an interesting way of saying it has given me more courage than you will ever know.

George and Jan Karam—for your encouragement and input, Uncle George. Aunt Jan, your citizenship is in heaven, and I eagerly await my Savior to one day take me to you.

Joy and Joe Wright—for listening to what I have to say, even when I talk for too long.

John Robertson, Jay Gragg, Becky and David Goodrum, and the whole Londonderry gang—for helping me pack and then loading my truck.

Tim O'Connor and Larry Young—for moving my stuff across

country! Your generosity will not be forgotten.

Dave and Anne Andis—for taking care of my home, packing my stuff, and generally being such great help to me.

Bill Jensen—for having the courage to say yes.

David Green—for the much-needed printer.

Judé and Joe Campofelice—for the computer.

Dr. Paul Looney, Pastor Dave Anderson, and Mark Keough— for your valuable input and encouragement in the early stages of this project.

Paul, Kacey, Jenni, Beth, Kim, and Debra—for generously sharing your stories.

The ORCA Crew—for being so patient with me.

Robert and Jayne Good—for joyfully giving me the freedom to share more of my story.

My editors at Multnomah—Keith Wall for not only having a brilliant editing eye, but for being a teacher and encourager as well; Dan Benson for your beautiful finesse with a pen; and Dr. Judith St. Pierre for not only reading my words, but for listening to my heart. I feel blessed to have such a skillful editing team.

My children, Erica, Louis, and Michael, the lights of my life— for your extreme patience and support for me while I wrote this book. Aren't you glad you don't have to hear the words "As soon as the book is finished" anymore? Mostly, though, I want to thank you for starting me on the road out of regret. I hope that one day you can fully understand just how much each of you means to me and how very much you are cherished.

Last and most importantly, thank you, my Father. This book is from You, through You, and to You. To You belong all glory, honor, and praise.

Part One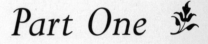

THE
TRAGEDY

Snowball Riding 101

Holding on for Dear Life

🌿 WE ALL have a story to tell. Yours might be simple or complex, dramatic or dull, predictable or adventurous; but because you picked up this book, it's a safe bet that regret is a part of it. Perhaps you've made unwise and unhealthy choices, and now you're suffering the consequences. You've tried to leave your past behind and move forward, but you just can't seem to do it. Let's face it: Regret doesn't let go easily. Nevertheless, I can say with confidence that it *is* possible to break free of it. I know because, like you, I have a story to tell.

Before my journey to regret began, I enjoyed an independent, confident, happy, healthy, and reasonably successful life. When it ended, I sat in my parents' house a hundred miles away from everything familiar—broke, jobless, homeless, humiliated, sick, and scared out of my mind.

My relatively predictable life had suddenly turned dramatic. Like a cartoon character riding a runaway snowball, I managed to stay on top for a while, but soon the snowball grew so huge and gained so much speed that it seemed to take on a life of its own. The momentum sucked me in and rolled me downhill at a dizzying pace. I felt out of control and helpless. When I inevitably crashed, I landed in a heap on my dad and stepmom's sofa.

In *A Comedy of Errors,* Shakespeare wrote, "For every why there is a wherefore." That was certainly true in my case. My ill-fated journey on the snowball didn't just begin on its own. It started with a series of decisions—all bad—that I made when I was about twenty years old.

I was supervising the advertising department of a company in Santa Cruz. It was the best job I'd ever had. I was learning a lot, enjoying it immensely, and I seemed to be on the fast track to success. I lived close to work and rented a room from my boyfriend's brother and his wife.

My boyfriend, Robert, attended college near San Francisco—almost a hundred miles north. We had been together for two years, and he had lived in San Francisco for half that time. The stress of being apart repeatedly strained our relationship to the breaking point. We were on-again, off-again for several months—on when he was around, off when he was away. Our relationship was passionate in every sense of the word. We argued intensely and often. Still, we were in love, and I hated the word *good-bye.*

Despite being separated from Robert, I felt happy, and, like many people just emerging from the teenage years, I had an attitude of invincibility. Emotionally, I considered myself in good shape. I didn't see the destructive patterns that had started popping up in my relationships. And though I was a Christian, my spiritual life was marked by apathy—I didn't sense my need for God.

Something was about to change all that.

The snow began to shift under my feet the day my boss announced that he was resigning from the company and moving to the East Coast. The news was an unwelcome surprise to me. I had enjoyed a professional, platonic relationship with my boss, who was ten years older than I and married. He had taken me under his wing and taught me a lot. We had forged a comfortable workplace friendship that I dreaded losing.

The thought of saying good-bye to my mentor caused me to panic. Evidently, he reacted the same way. We quietly began to leave notes expressing our sadness on each other's desks. As we tried to avoid the inevitable, those notes evolved into plans for an affair.

We spent a few days in Boston; we spent a few days in Atlanta. I told everyone, including my landlords, that I was traveling on business. Although Robert and I were in an "off-again" phase, I certainly didn't want to tell his brother the truth and risk having Robert hear it.

The affair ended quickly, bringing the dreaded good-bye. Within the month, I was back in San Francisco reconciling with Robert, and for a few weeks everything seemed normal. Then I decided to fly to Houston to visit my family. One evening I mentioned to my cousin that I was "late." I thought nothing about it, but she woke me up early the next morning and pulled me into the bathroom to take a pregnancy test.

The results were positive. When I read them, I crumpled to the floor. I couldn't have been more shocked. *Me,* pregnant? *Me,* an unwed mother? What would Robert say? What would my *father* say? I had been taught Christian values. Getting pregnant out of wedlock was simply not acceptable to my parents or me. To say that I felt devastated would be an understatement. My only solace came from the fact that my illicit relationship had remained a secret. Although *I* was certain that Robert was the father of this child, I shuddered to think what everyone else, including Robert, would think if they knew about the affair.

I called Robert from Houston and wept into the telephone, "I'm pregnant."

"Come home," he said instantly. "We'll get married."

We were obviously not ready for marriage, but his words and a hefty dose of unrealistic hope helped me regain my balance and stay atop my snowball. Somehow managing to hold things together, I flew home.

A few days later, after breaking the news of my pregnancy to my disappointed but supportive family, I went to work, only to hear the words, "You're fired." Again, I was shocked. I had performed my job well. But after my boss had quit, the power structure had shifted. My department went up for grabs, and unbeknownst to me, management had been looking for a way to fire me. When the news of my affair with my former boss leaked out, they had their reason to hand me a pink slip. My once tranquil life had suddenly turned into a soap opera.

With morning sickness and stress beginning to take their toll, I went home and crawled into bed. That weekend, Robert rode the train to Santa Cruz to visit and lend moral support. He sent me to relax in a hot bath while he spent time visiting with his brother and sister-in-law.

As I was getting out of the tub, I felt drained, weak, nauseous, and ill at ease. There was no sound in the house, and I sensed that something was wrong. Wearing only a towel, I rounded the corner of the hallway and stopped short at the sight of Robert holding some little yellow pieces of paper. One look at his face confirmed my fear—something was indeed wrong. He had gone into my room looking for matches, but instead he found the notes from my former boss. I was caught. Robert was crushed. His face twisted in disbelief, pain, and fury as he read the notes aloud—not only for me to hear, but for his brother and sister-in-law as well.

When he finished, he hissed through clenched teeth, "Get dressed. You're taking me home—*now*."

Humiliated and scared, I quickly obeyed.

Because he had taken the train to Santa Cruz, driving my car was the only immediate way back to San Francisco. So we spent two hours driving north, sometimes in painful discussion, sometimes in agonizing silence. I hated that he hurt, but in a way, I felt relieved that he knew. As bizarre as it sounds given my actions, I didn't want us to have any secrets when—or if—we got married. Since I didn't seem to have anything more to lose, I answered honestly as he angrily fired question after question at me. But he didn't ask just about my affair with my boss. He also questioned me about another relationship I'd had several years earlier. I had previously lied about it; now I chose to tell the truth.

Hearing it sent Robert over the edge. He was furious, and

rightly so. Fuming, he abruptly pulled off the freeway, left me in the car, walked to a pay phone, and called my parents. He told them to come get me at his house because he'd "had enough."

I spent the next week trying to explain myself to my family, my boyfriend, and—because she'd also discovered the truth—the wife of my former boss.

My snowball had crashed. In less than two weeks' time, I discovered that I was pregnant, got engaged, got fired, got caught, got dumped, and got evicted. I was a mess—a mess with morning sickness.

My journey into regret had officially begun.

JUST FORGET IT AND MOVE ON?

Believe it or not, over the next several years I continued to make life-altering mistakes. My Christian upbringing compounded my guilt. I was supposed to know better. And because I was a believer, I was supposed to have the power to *do* better.

Charles Spurgeon once wrote:

> I have endured tribulation from many flails. Sharp bodily pain succeeded mental depression, and this was accompanied both by bereavement and affliction in the person of one dear as life. The waters rolled in continually, wave upon wave. I do not mention this to exact sympathy, but simply to let the reader see that I am no dry-land sailor. I have traversed those oceans which are not Pacific full many a time: I know the roll of the billows, and the rush of the winds.[1]

Like Spurgeon, I address the subject of regret as one who has been there and hasn't forgotten how it feels to be humbled by failure. I am not writing as one who has avoided all major mistakes in life, but as one who has fallen—headlong—into most of them.

Every time I made a new blunder, I asked God to forgive me and tried to put my past behind me. But the consternation I felt consisted of much more than guilt, so seeking forgiveness wasn't enough. I was stuck with miserable feelings of regret and remorse. When I sought answers to my despair, I was often told, "That's water under the bridge"; "No sense crying over spilled milk"; and "Give it to God." Though well-meaning, such expressions were useless. I carried on, but I was not consoled.

If regrets plague you, you know as well as I do that phrases like "Just forget it and move on" and "You'll forget in time" don't work. We can't "forget in time" because time doesn't heal every wound. If we can't get past our past, we will never stop thinking about it, especially if we continue to suffer the consequences of it. If we can't remove regret from our hearts, we will never experience inner peace.

The immediate consequences of my snowball crash made it pretty hard to "just forget it." I had to endure months of lonely silence until Robert was certain that our child was indeed *our* child. It was hard to stop regretting getting pregnant out of wedlock when I was acutely aware of others looking at my swollen belly and then at the ringless finger of my left hand. It was tough to get Robert's pained look or that devastated wife's tortured voice out of my head. The things I regretted were things I had done that had irreversibly changed the course of my life and the lives of other people. How could I "just forget" them?

Sometimes how we feel about our mistakes can have more

consequences than the mistakes themselves. For instance, I have a friend who was sorry that she had married the man she did, but instead of seeking to love her husband in spite of his faults, she made herself miserable with endless "if onlys." She also made her husband miserable with her obvious dissatisfaction. Divorce came, and sorrows multiplied. Her entire family suffered. Her snowball gained speed. When it finally crashed, she was left, like me, with even more regret, feelings of hopelessness, and nothing but clichés for comfort.

DO YOU HOPE, OR DO YOU HOPE NOT?

In the movie *Pleasantville,* a couple of average teenagers from the '90s are magically pulled into their television set and find themselves in the town of Pleasantville in the '50s. There, they try to cope in a black-and-white and nauseatingly pleasant world. What makes it so monochromatic and sickeningly sweet is that nothing unexpected ever happens, and nothing ever goes wrong. Everybody's words and schedules are scripted. Politeness is ever present, and failure doesn't exist.

Only when the new kids in town stir things up by not acting according to the script does color begin to appear in Pleasantville. Many of the townspeople are thrown into turmoil. They don't know how to function in a world that isn't orderly and predictable. At one point in the movie, the skin of a character much like June Cleaver takes on a pinkish hue. Though she is secretly excited by the color, she fears disapproval, so she applies gray makeup in order to remain acceptable to others.

Sadly, some of the characters in the movie believe that fun and color are synonymous with sin. The rest of them believe that sin irrevocably destroys the story. In fact, there doesn't seem to be one character in *Pleasantville* who depicts the truth.

When we have debilitating regret, we are like those Pleasantville residents who believed that sin hopelessly ruined the story. We want our lives to go according to the script we've written in our minds. When it doesn't, we're thrown into turmoil. We anguish over how our lives have changed and how they appear to others. We fear what others will think of us, so like the June Cleaver character, we try to undo what has been done in order to fit back into a world where things are supposed to be "just so."

How I would have loved to undo my past! I liked having everything black and white, but the things I had done had made things too "colorful." To apply a little gray and be the perfect Christian girl would have been wonderful compared to dealing with the aftermath of my shameful choices.

When our remorse is relentless, we are like the other group of Pleasantville characters—not as they were in the film, believing that sin is what makes life enjoyable—but as they would have been had the story continued, which, thankfully, it didn't. Those characters weren't far from discovering that self-reproach creates a colorless world all its own. Regret is a vacuum that sucks all the joy out of life. It affects every sense God has given us to enjoy Him and His blessings.

It diminishes the spiritual senses first. When we live under its condemnation, it becomes difficult to see, hear, taste, touch, or smell the things of God. Soon it impairs even the physical senses, and when that happens, all the joy drains from our existence. When we harbor regret, we end up in a place much like Pleasantville—minus the pleasantness. We live in a totally colorless, dull gray, joyless world. Ironically, instead of comforting us, a black-and-white existence frustrates us, because the lack of joy depletes our strength and makes it easy for us to lose hope.

How about you? Do you think that past mistakes have ruined the story of your life? Does your life feel colorless, dull, and passionless because of regret? Have you lost hope? It doesn't have to be that way—no matter what your past looks like. I hope that the principles in this book will help you find the joy and excitement that your regret has stolen. I know that they can bring healing, because they have done so in my own life.

I used to live under a cloud of anxiety because of regret. As I looked at my life through its dull gray lens, I felt hopeless. Although I examined my circumstances from every angle, thinking them out and praying them through, I found no way to change them. My life seemed futile, and I felt angry—angry with myself for failing, with others for failing me, and with God for failing to rescue me from myself and others. I wanted Him to step into my world and stop my snowball from careening downhill. When He didn't, I wanted Him to explain Himself. Basically, I was pouting.

Anger wasn't my only problem. When I looked at friends who had sins in their past and saw that they had happy lives and successful ministries and that they rejoiced in their freedom, I became jealous. It appeared that their sins, unlike mine, hadn't been so bad that their lives were devastated. It seemed so unfair. I felt envious and hopeless because they had what I wanted but believed I could never have—God's best.

What's worse, regret paralyzed me, making me unable to serve God or fully love others. I tried to cope, but of course I did it the wrong way. I consistently sought relief from my pain instead of relationship with God. It was not only a self-centered way to live, but it also led to more regret.

For several years I continued struggling with various difficulties that resulted either from my mistakes or the remorse I felt in their wake. Eventually I realized that I needed to seek bibical counseling for one-on-one help in applying God's Word to my debilitating pain. That kind of help, however, wasn't an option when I needed it, because I simply couldn't afford it.

So I began to search God's Word on my own. I realized that there was no better Counselor than the Holy Spirit and that He was available twenty-four hours a day, seven days a week, for free. I didn't just *read* the Bible, though; I studied it in depth with the help of good teachers and good books. I asked and trusted God to help me apply His Word to my personal situation. I asked Him to set me free from the chains of my past.

As God applied truth to my life, I began to see positive changes. Through His Word, I discovered that it was possible to move from regret to a hopeful anticipation of the future. Despite my disastrous journey on the snowball I had created, His Word enabled me to pick myself up, dust off the snow, and get past my past. It gave me the courage to dare.

I dared to believe that God meant what He said in these Scriptures:

- "The thief comes only to steal and kill and destroy; I have come that they may have life, and have it to the full." (John 10:10)
- "I have told you this so that my joy may be in you and that your joy may be complete." (John 15:11)

- He who did not spare his own Son, but gave him up for us all—how will he not also, along with him, graciously give us all things? (Romans 8:32)

I dared to believe that God was *that* gracious and that those Scriptures were God's will for my life. I dared to believe that there was productive, joyful life beyond regret, despite how I felt. And since an abundant life was God's will for me, I dared to believe that He had made a provision for me to attain it, despite my past mistakes.

Perhaps your heart is heavy with regret. Perhaps you've heard all the clichés about "getting on with your life," when what you've needed to hear is how to get past your past. Perhaps you've never heard that there is a way to resolve the guilt, shame, and pain that you feel. Perhaps God has resurrected you from your dead past, but you still find yourself in a colorless world, lacking joy and gladness. Or perhaps, like Lazarus, you're alive and have stepped out of the tomb, but you're still wearing grave clothes (see John 11:38–44). If any of these statements ring true about you, it's time to hear some good news.

It's time to look deeply into God's Word to see what He has to say about failure, regret, and redemption. It's time to accept that He wants to take you by the hand and lift you out of the pit of remorse. It's time to believe that His promises are true and offered to you regardless of what you have done in the past.

HOPE FOR WHAT?

When I needed help getting past my past, I didn't find anything on the bookshelf to help me apply God's Word to my regret. *Getting*

Past Your Past is my attempt to share, from my own experience, the truths I learned about the wonderful, healing grace of a God who cares.

I know that, with God's help, you can break the power of the "if onlys" in your life.

I know that you can truly put those things that cause regret behind you.

I know that God has provided a way, as Paul said in Philippians 3:13–14, to forget what is behind and press on.

Frederick Buechner once said, "Sometimes wishing is the wings the truth comes true on. Sometimes the truth is what sets us wishing for it."[2] My wish is that *Getting Past Your Past* will make you hungry for the truths of God's Word, the Bread of Life. I pray that it will help you find hope and a joyful, abundant life despite your failures—and maybe, in some ways, even because of them.

2

"If Only..."

Stuck in the Muck

❧ "IF ONLY..." How many times have you said those words?

Often we say them and then mentally complete the sentence to revise history—as if everything would have, could have, and should have been okay. No, I take that back—we don't usually settle for *okay* when we're in the throes of a good rewrite. Instead, we revise the past to include an ideal outcome. We might say, "Oh, if *only* I hadn't gotten divorced! By now we'd have 2.4 children and be living in our dream house in the country. John would come home from work and play ball with the kids while I cooked dinner...which would be a joy because I wouldn't have to work outside the home...which means I'd be three sizes smaller because

I wouldn't have to sit at this desk all day...."

On and on the fantasy goes. The more we fill in the "if onlys" with dreamy scenarios, the deeper we sink into the muck of regret. True, imagining a different life for ourselves gives us a little relief from the pain of our past—at least momentarily. Fantasizing about what life *could have been* feels like a soothing balm on our wounds of remorse. When reality bites, escaping into the dreamworld of wistful thinking is sometimes the Calgon that takes us away when we can't quite make it to the bathtub.

Sometimes.

Other times, those nagging "if onlys" torment us. "If only I hadn't gotten divorced, I wouldn't have messed up God's plan for my life." Regret becomes the accuser that won't let us rest. It says, "You messed up. You can't change the past...but you sure better die trying." So we try. We try to undo our mistakes, cover them up, or sidestep their consequences. When that proves futile, we try to find ways to cope, but these efforts, too, end only in more pain, frustration, and regret.

When I say *regret,* I'm not talking about the good kind—the healthy, God-given remorse that breaks our hearts, bends our knees in confession, and brings us in repentance to the Lord. If regret is functioning properly, it will cause us to make things right with God and, where appropriate, with any human beings our actions have affected. But once we have confessed, repented, and made restitution for our actions, *regret will leave us.* If it lingers, we may be experiencing what the apostle Paul called worldly sorrow: "Godly sorrow brings repentance that leads to salvation and *leaves no regret, but worldly sorrow brings death*" (2 Corinthians 7:10, emphasis added). God wants us to confess and repent of our sins. Even when we do so, He may require that we endure the consequences of our actions. He does not, however, intend that we feel perpetually miserable.

So how does worldly sorrow come into our lives? Regret begins when we fail—when we act in a way that is contrary to God's guidance and revealed will. We lie. We cheat. We refuse to forgive. We mismanage anger. We aren't good parents. In a later chapter, we'll discuss the main reasons we fail and how we can avoid failing and, therefore, avoid regret. For now, let's focus on the fact that when we fail—when we sin, make mistakes, or miss opportunities—we often end up suffering consequences and harboring regret.

SWAMPED WITH GUILT: THE COMPONENTS OF REGRET

Regret reminds us repeatedly of what we know all too well: There is a point of no return. There is a time when it's too late to have or do what we want. We can't always replace a lost fortune or mend a marriage. We can't nullify an illicit affair, reverse an abortion, or put fired bullets back in the gun barrel. Regret hounds us if we never get past these truths. Realizing that we can't undo mistakes, we have difficulty looking beyond the failure to the future. Facing the consequences of sin and suffering and the pain of knowing that we did it to ourselves, we get stuck in the muck of regret.

When we become fixated on our poor choices and failures, certain things drag us into the quicksand of regret. Let's look briefly at five of them. (We'll discuss each one in more detail in the chapters to come.)

Guilt

Our sin may be huge, with terrible repercussions affecting many people, or it may be "not that bad" by some standards. It doesn't matter. We still feel guilty for the pain we've caused others and ourselves. Often our guilt is magnified because we thought that we never would have done such a thing—and we were wrong. Or our pain is increased because we know how to *be* forgiven but not how to *feel* forgiven.

Unresolved guilt is a slippery slope into the quagmire of condemnation. But how can we resolve it when we cannot fix what we've done? A paradox, isn't it?

Secrets

When we blow it, we usually feel fear—and rightly so, for chastisement follows failure. We learn this in a number of ways: Disobey Mom and be grounded; lie to Dad and receive a spanking; talk back to the teacher and be marched to the principal's office; drive too fast and get a ticket; break the company's rules and be reprimanded or fired.

We learn from experience to fear the pain and embarrassment of reproof. So when we mess up, we often do everything we can to avoid reproach. The more fear we feel, the more extreme our measures of self-protection. We cover up. We hide. We keep secrets. We lie. We isolate ourselves. And we stay afraid.

Anger and Unforgivingness

Sometimes our mistakes are 100 percent our fault. But often, other people have negatively affected our decision-making ability. We know that we're supposed to forgive those who have influenced our bad choices, but we're too angry and hurt. We don't feel like for-giving them, and praying hasn't changed that fact. We certainly don't want to be reconciled to them only to be victimized again. We want them to hear our outraged cry of pain, but we feel like we're screaming into deaf ears.

We've had enough of whoever caused our pain. Unfortunately, we often can't escape them. Sometimes they live with us. Unless we let go of our anger and forgive whoever has hurt us, we're sure to stay mired in regret.

Misconceptions about God

Most of us have misconceptions about God. And when we don't know the truth about Him, we're sure to make mistakes and suffer the consequences, one of which is regret. If nothing else, hasn't our endless remorse taught us that? Still, how can the truth help us now? God wanted the best for us. He had a plan, but we blew it. Now there's no going back. Haven't we frustrated Him and His intentions? So why didn't He prevent this disaster in the first place? And how will He ever fix this mess now? What if He doesn't? Even if He does, our life will always be a shadow of what it could have been—right? How we answer these questions reveals our under-standing of God, and how we understand God will largely deter-mine our ability to overcome regret.

Failure to Grieve Loss

Sin brings consequences, and many times they come in the form of things we lose—a promising career, a marriage, a child, a friendship. The pain of loss makes us think, *It didn't have to be this way* and *This can't be right; this hurts too much.* When we fail to grieve our losses—

to recognize and accept them—we stay stuck in the muck of regret.

Accompanying the pain of loss is the fear that it will never subside. When I am in pain, I want relief. When I can't undo whatever I did that is causing my pain, I'm sucked even further into the quicksand by renewed guilt, anger, grief, frustration, and hopelessness.

LIVING TO REGRET IT: PAUL AND KACEY

Some people spend years suffering not only from the effects of their actions, but also from the effects of regret itself. They end up feeling as if they have wasted years of their lives. Sound familiar? It does to Paul and Kacey.

🌿 WHEN PAUL was thirty-eight years old, he made a decision that he ended up regretting for more than a decade. He was living a comfortable, moderate lifestyle in Kansas with his wife, teenage daughter, and young son, when some family members asked him to become part owner of a lucrative business they had started in New York. Paul was excited. From all indications, the business would only grow, and he would make a fortune.

But investing in the business and working for the company meant that the family had to move from financially stable circumstances in familiar Kansas to a risky situation in unfamiliar New York. Paul's wife, Mary, and their children were less than thrilled with the idea. They didn't want to move. Mary, especially, sensed that it was a bad idea. In time, Paul's blind enthusiasm won her over, and Mary agreed to go, but she insisted that Paul set aside some funds in case the jackpot he was hoping for didn't materialize. If they stashed away some money, she told him, they could at least move back to Kansas and buy a home. Paul agreed that it was the wise thing to do—but somehow he never did it.

Almost immediately after moving to New York, Paul realized that his dream didn't square with reality. The business in which he had invested his life savings required him to work twelve hours a day, six days a week. He was exhausted. Mary was lonely. The family began to feel the strain of an absent father, a depressed mother, and the jarring adjustment of moving from Kansas to New York. None of them liked it.

At the end of a difficult year, the business failed, in part because of the dishonest practices of some of the family members Paul had trusted—the same family members who had convinced him to join the business. Not only did Paul lose every penny of his savings, but the IRS also demanded that he personally pay the company's taxes because he had been a company officer and the company check-signer.

As soon as he could, Paul scraped together enough money to move the family back to Kansas. They arrived with nothing except their furniture and clothes. When they had left Kansas, they had sold a nice, three-bedroom house in a middle-class neighborhood. When they returned, they rented a cramped, ramshackle old house in a bad part of town. It was all they could afford.

Paul's family endured humiliation in their community as they faced the friends, neighbors, and church members who knew about their failure. The move proved especially painful for the children, as Paul's son was entering the socially challenging time of junior high school, and his daughter was entering her first year of college. Paul returned to Kansas, as he says, "with my tail between my legs."

When Paul realized that the desire to get rich quick had motivated him to invest the family's money, he began to sink in the quicksand of remorse. He regretted uprooting his family against their will, getting them into such painful circumstances, and not providing for them. He reproached himself for not listening to his wife and for contributing to her deep depression. It would be years before Paul would again trust his decision-making ability—years before he would recover emotionally and financially from the regret of that one bad decision.

🌿 KACEY WAS only eighteen years old the first time she stepped into a strip bar. She says, "My first thought was, *Oh, no! I can't be in here, I'm not old enough!*" It was a go-go bar where the dancing girls wore bikinis. Kacey was with a group of new friends and was eager for their acceptance, so she tried to relax by having a few drinks. With the alcohol loosening her up and distorting her judgment, it wasn't long before her thinking changed.

"Suddenly, I wasn't thinking about how young I was," she recalls. "I thought, *Hey, if those girls can do it, so can I! It kind of looks like fun!*"

About that time, the manager of the bar approached Kacey and asked if she'd like to give dancing a try. She was afraid, but agreed anyway. "So in my jeans and T-shirt, I hopped up on the stage and danced my little heart out. The men flocked to the stage to give me tips and compliments. I'd never felt that good about myself!"

Kacey spent the rest of the night in the bathroom sick from alcohol, which she wasn't accustomed to drinking. When she woke up late the next morning, she felt confused about what she'd done.

She called a friend to confess. But in the middle of her confession, she started pulling the money out of her pockets, and something inside her clicked.

"I suddenly knew this was something I could do," she says. "After all, I reasoned, the girls wore bikinis. I wore those all summer long, so what was the big deal? This new venture offered me money, attention, acceptance, fun, and more compliments than I could possibly imagine."

Of course, there was a small battle with her conscience. Kacey had accepted Christ four years earlier while attending a youth group activity at a friend's church. But in time, the enthusiasm for her faith wore off, and she went looking for something more exciting. Go-go dancing certainly fit the bill.

Kacey had always shown a pattern of needing more and more excitement and adventure to keep her satisfied. It didn't take long dancing in the bikini bar for her to be intrigued by the prospect of dancing in less clothing for more money a little farther outside the city limits. Kacey recalls, "My money intake doubled, but so did the danger for me. Not only the danger of what could happen to me at night, but also the danger of Satan's demons taking me by the hand and leading me deeper and deeper into their pit."

Then one night at a church event, Kacey felt caught in the middle of a spiritual tug-of-war. It was a father-daughter banquet, and her dad had asked her to attend with him. Kacey went because she lacked, and badly needed, a close relationship with her father.

"I recall sitting next to my dad and yearning to be his little girl again—but not only my earthly father's daughter," she says. "My heavenly Father was also calling His prodigal child home. I remember *aching* to come back to church. But then I looked over and saw a regular customer from the bar where I was working. He winked at me from across the room as if to say, 'I won't tell if you won't.' Immediately, all thoughts of returning to the Lord left me."

Not long after that, Kacey grew bored again and decided to move "up" in the stripping world. She became one of the main attractions at the most popular strip bar in her city. With her new job came new friends and a new feature in her lifestyle—drugs.

Just before her nineteenth birthday, Kacey attended her first all-night cocaine party. It turned out to be one of many as she began to rely more and more on drugs to cope with her inner turmoil. "I kept trying to find peace and something to fill the emptiness I felt inside," she says. Her drug habit got so severe that she began dealing in drugs to support it.

It wasn't long until Kacey's lifestyle resulted in an unplanned pregnancy. At the urging of her boyfriend and against her conscience, she made an appointment at an abortion clinic. But while she was on the table undergoing a preabortion sonogram, she heard a gasp from the nurse who was scanning the monitor. Kacey quickly turned and saw two fetuses on the screen. Immediately, she pulled on her clothes, grabbed her purse, and ran out of the clinic. She couldn't go through with the abortion knowing she was carrying twins.

A month later, on New Year's Eve, 1990, Kacey miscarried the babies. "You would think that would have been a perfect opportunity to turn and follow God's voice," she said. "Instead, I chose to continue wasting years in foolish behavior."

After the miscarriage, Kacey's lifestyle of stripping and drug use continued uninterrupted until the spring of 1992, when she again found herself pregnant—this time by a different boyfriend. The

child's father abandoned Kacey. This time she
abortion, and she stopped stripping and doing
to give birth to a healthy boy.

Becoming a single mother was only the firs .... shocks
for Kacey. Over the next few months, her heart was broken into
pieces. First, only moments after stepping out of a car that carried
two of her friends, Kacey turned to wave good-bye and then
watched as the passenger side of the car where her best friend sat
was demolished by a drunk driver going seventy miles an hour. Her
friend died instantly. Not long after that tragedy, one of Kacey's
coworkers was beaten to death by her husband, another was murdered by a stranger, and a third was stalked by a man who kid-
napped, tortured, and then murdered her.

Badly shaken, Kacey decided that it was time to get out of the
lifestyle that had brought her nothing but heartache and regret. She
knew that it was time to find a way out of her cycle of pain. Finally,
she stopped stripping, quit using drugs, and began the long journey back to wholeness in God.

MIRED IN THE AFTERMATH:
THE CYCLE OF REGRET

The personal consequences of unresolved *regret* can be just as devastating as the effects of sin. As Paul and Kacey discovered, regret
leaves powerful emotions in its wake, and if they are not dealt with,
they will often lead to more poor choices and sin. Unless regret is
resolved in the proper way—through confession, repentance, and
relationship with God—we will most often seek relief from our
pain in ways that produce more regret. The cycle usually goes like

ɔ. An initial sin or mistake leads to regret...which is followed by some destructive coping mechanism...which brings more sin and mistakes...which prompts more regret. On and on the downward spiral goes.

Kacey was caught in that cycle of regret, and it took a series of tragedies before she finally quit stripping and using drugs. Feeling guilt and anguish for her initial decision to start stripping, she had turned to drugs to escape her inner pain. But her drug use led to even more destructive choices (illicit sex, more serious drug use, drug dealing), which led to more regret, which led to a more frantic search for relief.

Of course, not everyone turns to drugs for comfort. Some turn to alcohol, overeating, gambling, pornography, escapism, or inappropriate relationships. When we rely on these things to cope with guilt and hopelessness, we find that regret begets regret—and the cycle continues.

Sometimes we move forward in our journey only to be pulled back. We confess our misdeeds, ask for forgiveness, and try desperately to move on with our lives. Then come what I call the "naysayers" to thwart our progress. These usually appear in one of three forms: our own self-recriminating thoughts; other people, who insist on reminding us of our failures; and the evil one, Satan, the "accuser of [the] brethren" (Revelation 12:10, NASB).

To fend off these naysayers, we must learn the truth and overcome the regret that plagues us. When we do, encouraging words of healing will replace the discouraging words we say to ourselves. We must also learn to tell others the truth in love, reminding them that no one is flawless and that God offers forgiveness to everyone. And lastly, we have to tell Satan to buzz off. As someone once said,

"When Satan reminds you of your past, remind him of his future," which is the lake of fire (Revelation 20:10). When he holds something over your head, remind him that your past is under your feet—as he will be soon (Romans 16:20).

One of the most pervasive naysayers is the message—from our own mind, the words of others, or Satan—that we have let God down. A friend once told me, "Satan is not my problem. It's guilt because I've disappointed God. I can't get over the feeling that I've let Him down."

God certainly desires our obedience, and He grieves when we don't obey. The apostle Paul said, "Do not grieve the Holy Spirit of God, with whom you were sealed for the day of redemption" (Ephesians 4:30). God has a high standard; He wants us to "be perfect…as your heavenly father is perfect" (Matthew 5:48). Yet the Bible affirms that all of us have sinned and fallen short of God's standard (Romans 3:23). That's why He sent His only Son. Through Jesus' death on the cross, we can be reconciled to God and have *abundant* life. We don't dash God's expectations with our errors, for if we could, we would also be able to raise His hopes with our righteousness. When we say, "I've let God down," it sounds like we have surprised Him with our failures. Our heavenly Father isn't surprised by anything.

Still, it's no small thing to think that you've dashed the expectations of the King of heaven and earth. I know. I used to feel that way. At one time in my life, I felt locked in a prison of pain. I thought that I had let God down and permanently messed up His plan for my life. I didn't think that it was possible for my dreams to become a reality. The feeling that I had forever disappointed God and destroyed His plan for me kept me mired in regret for a long time. The feeling began after my first big snowball crash, but it grew stronger as I continued to make more mistakes.

My cycle of regret began when Robert found out about my affair with my former boss. Although I was pregnant with Robert's child, he and I spent an entire year away from each other. During that time, I had only to renew my relationship with the Lord, prepare for the birth of my first child, and then take care of my new daughter, Erica. But while my pain led me to realize the importance of renewing my relationship with God, it did little to actually get me relating to Him. I passionately believed in Jesus, but I still didn't passionately follow Him.

In 1985, when Erica was five months old, Robert and I reconciled. We married three months later. Looking back now, it's easy to see that neither of us was ready for the sacrifices marriage would demand. I spent more of our brief marriage *preaching to* Robert than I did *loving* him. My passion was misplaced. Despite my sincere declarations of faith, I lacked the dedication to the Lord that leads to love. And according to 1 Corinthians 13:1 a lack of love made me nothing but a "resounding gong or a clanging cymbal" to my husband. Our marriage died a quick and extremely painful death.

At that time in my life, I made choices based on how good they made me feel. Therefore, after Robert and I split up it wasn't long before I jumped into another relationship and then marriage because it "felt right." My new husband, Marty, and I were in the same situation when we married. We both carried baggage from recent, painful, unresolved relationships and we both struggled with anger, bitterness, fear, and insecurity. It wasn't long before the consequences of marrying "on the rebound" set in—and with them came regret.

The next few years were an emotional roller coaster ride. I was filled with joy at the births of two sons, Louis and Michael; but I was also filled with depression as I tried to cope with all of my new responsibilities. Marty and I each had children from our previous marriages. My Erica was just a toddler; Marty's two children, Jay and Becky, were preteens. I became an instant and often full-time step-mom to two children who were angry about their father's divorce.

The weight of those difficult relationships was sometimes so crushing that it seemed obvious to me that Marty and I had stepped outside of God's will when we married. I was convinced that I had disappointed God and irreversibly thwarted His plan for my life. I was told not to despair, because even if I had thwarted God's plan, He always had another plan—plan B. Still, I wasn't comforted because I couldn't recover from the guilt of having destroyed plan A.

That guilt, along with the fear that I would also wreck plan B, motivated me to persevere in my marriage to Marty and to be a good mother and stepmother to my five children. We forged ahead as a family, sometimes happily, sometimes painfully, but over seven years we slowly grew in faith and unity.

During those seven years we moved to Texas to follow a job opportunity for Marty and to be near my extended family. In the fall of 1994—when Jay and Becky had almost completed their teen years, Erica was nine, Louis six, and Michael four—our lives took a dramatic turn.

First, I fell in our backyard and ruptured a disc in my back, an injury that required two months of bed rest followed by major surgery. Three weeks after the operation, while I was still recovering, my mother called from California to tell me that she had incurable lung cancer. Four weeks later, Marty was diagnosed with incurable malignant melanoma—skin cancer. Our family was devastated.

Within a year, I was a motherless widow with two shattered teenagers and three frightened children. Compounding my grief was my belief that I had messed up God's plan for my life. I wrestled with significant questions: *If I had followed God's path instead of my own, how would things be different? If this is God's plan B for my life, what would plan A have looked like? Besides, what will I do as a single mother? How can I care for and support these children?* At the same time that I was processing the loss of my husband and mother, I was paralyzed by regret.

BOGGED IN THE QUAGMIRE: THE PARALYSIS OF REGRET

Often we don't recognize that regret is the source of our paralysis because its symptoms are often the same as those of many other problems. Regret can manifest itself in a number of ways. Some of the most common are:

- depression
- fear
- a constant sense of failure
- a lack of joy
- a lack of purpose
- emotional numbness
- spiritual apathy
- envy of those who do have dreams and goals and the ability to realize them

Another common and critical symptom of regret is *waiting to live*. We wait for our circumstances to change so that we can "get on with life," but sometimes we're waiting for something that will never come because the consequences of our regret are permanent. So we keep ourselves in a constant state of confusion because we reside neither in the past nor in the present. And plans for the future? Forget it. We end up in a perpetual holding pattern, and precious time goes by that we can never recapture. We're like the understudy in a play who is always rehearsing but never performing, perpetually waiting in the wings but never on stage. We can know we're forgiven and yet, like me, still be waiting until we feel "right" before we set a goal or seek to serve.

Jesus said that believers are the "salt of the earth" (Matthew 5:13). We are supposed to be seasoning our world with love, hope, grace, and service. Believers in Christ are His bride. Unfortunately, the bride of Christ is often like the bride of Lot—a frozen pillar of salt. And how did she become that pillar of salt? By looking back when she should have been moving forward (see Genesis 19).

Jesus used Lot's wife as an example when He was making one of His favorite points: "Remember Lot's wife! Whoever tries to keep his life will lose it, and whoever loses his life will preserve it" (Luke 17:32–33). Looking back was Lot's wife's way of trying to hold on to her past life. When we as part of the bride of Christ look back at what was or what might have been, we suffer the same fate. We become frozen and ineffective.

Not only is the church the bride of Christ, but we are also His body—Christ at work in the physical world. Just as regret affects each of us as individuals, it also affects the church as a whole because our ineffectualness affects others. When Christians act like the walking wounded, we weaken the body of Christ, and its work suffers. If our regret leads us to believe that we have failed beyond redemption or repair, we leave the serving to those we think are more qualified. Then, indeed, "the workers are few" (Matthew 9:37).

Because I felt that way for a long time, I began studying the Bible to see if I could find out how good I had to be to serve God. I was relieved by what I found. Two of my favorite characters, Moses and Peter, served God the most *after* their greatest failures. Moses had murdered a man and fled Egypt before God called him to free the Israelites. And though Peter was a born leader, it was only after he had been "sifted as wheat" by Satan, and then restored, that the Lord entrusted him with the responsibility of leading and encouraging his brothers. It is when we know who we really are and how utterly dependent we are on God that we best serve Him. That is why Christians who have failed and been properly restored are often the most useful in the Lord's work.

Regret doesn't just affect our ability to serve; it also affects our ability to relate to God and to other people. Getting bogged down in unresolved guilt, secrets, anger, unforgivingness, unbelief, or grief strains all our relationships. Jesus said that the two most important things in life are to love God and to love other people (Mark 12:29–31). Therefore, the worst result of regret isn't that we don't serve the Lord effectively; it's that we don't love Him or our neighbors sufficiently. Regret impedes relationships, and since Jesus said that relationships are what life is all about, regret truly is a tragedy.

All of us need to understand that just because we have regrets doesn't mean that God sees us as less important, less useful, or less lovable. We are all God-gifted, necessary parts of the body of

Christ. Nevertheless, lingering regret dims our vision and hinders the exercise of our gifts. We all have something to give; we just can't see it from where we are. And we all desperately need to have intimate relationships with God and others. For these reasons, it's imperative that we move beyond failure to restoration.

Thankfully, both Paul and Kacey did so.

With the help of two good friends who offered assistance and accountability, Paul recovered financially and spiritually. In faith, he clung to the Lord and eventually rose above his regret.

Kacey left her destructive lifestyle and returned to the Lord in repentance. I met her when she was serving the Lord at a large conference for women. As I listened to her story, I was thrilled to hear that after she had married and recommitted herself to Christ, she once again received the joyful news that she was pregnant—with twins. They were born healthy and happy in the summer of 1996.

You might know someone who, like Paul and Kacey, desperately needs to be freed from regret in order to dream a dream and serve the Lord. Maybe that someone is you. Several years ago, that someone was me. The journey out of regret isn't always easy, but it's always worth it.

Like all journeys, it begins with a single step, and when we take it, we quickly realize that we're not alone. If we carry stones with us to throw at our fellow travelers, we'll find it harder to reach our destination. So the first thing we need to do is to get rid of the baggage of condemnation.

3

No Stone to Throw

Bedrock Truth for the Journey

🌿 "AT THE time, I didn't think that what I said was cocky. I was serious. It was my birthday and a huge one at that. I had waited a long time to become a teenager. So when the day finally arrived, I was feeling both nostalgic and expectant—looking back at the passing of my youth and forward to the coming of my driver's license.

Okay, the truth is, I was feeling a little more than that. I was feeling…well…larger than life. I was thirteen, and *I* had arrived. I sat on the edge of my bed across from my dresser mirror, looked straight into my own eyes, and said out loud with great sincerity (I am not making this up), "Now I know *everything*."

Funny thing about knowing everything—it makes you stupid. That is, I spent much of the remainder of my teen years saying yes to bad things and no to good ones. "Drugs? Sure." "College? No, thanks." My pride not only didn't serve me well, it also nearly obliterated the "good girl" image I had carefully cultivated.

What my teenage mind had yet to grasp was that apart from the Lord, even my greatest strengths could turn into weaknesses. Without the Lord's strength, nothing that I had—not knowledge, experience, talent, or a positive attitude—could save me from failing miserably. Since all of us have weaknesses, and since all of us at some point choose to disregard the strength available to us through God, failure is universal.

That seems like an obvious truth—as the saying goes, "Nobody's perfect." But for a long time I felt hopeless because I thought that I was worse than others. I knew intellectually that "all have sinned and fall short of the glory of God" (Romans 3:23), but I felt that I had "fallen shorter" than most. I would mentally categorize people: Those like me who had failed publicly or in an egregiously unacceptable way were *bad* sinful, while everyone else was just *normal* sinful. This distinction only compounded my sense of condemnation, keeping me mired in a regret-filled life.

When we begin measuring ourselves against other people, we establish a pattern of condemnation. When we conclude that some people are better than we are, we will inevitably think that others are worse. If we examine people's lives superficially, we can always find reasons to judge them. But grace demands that we take a deeper look—as I eventually learned when I took a closer look at the life of a Jewish fisherman named Peter.

THE ROCKY ROAD TO REGRET

When I first read about Peter, I found it easy to think that his story was different from mine. He was in a privileged position of leadership. Right off the bat my expectations for him were high. He was, after all, a disciple. He literally walked by the Lord's side and talked with Him face-to-face. If I had had the Lord right at my side like Peter did, surely I would have been stronger. I mean, he received instruction from Jesus up close and personal. How could he possibly go on to blow it? He should have known better, right? He did know better, which makes it even easier to judge him. Jesus warned Peter no fewer than three times that he was about to face a huge test.

The first time was during the Last Supper. "Simon, Simon," the Lord said, "Satan has asked to sift you as wheat" (Luke 22:31). Those are daunting words coming from Jesus! I used to think that if Jesus had said that to me, I'd have been looking for Satan's trap around every corner.

Jesus' second warning came right after the first, when He spelled out the situation for Peter. Interestingly, He did it in response to Peter's passionate declarations of loyalty. Peter proudly announced that even if all the other disciples abandoned Jesus, he would not. He went so far as to say that he was ready to die for Christ. He wasn't, of course, and Jesus told him so. "'I tell you the truth,' Jesus answered, 'this very night, before the rooster crows, you will disown me three times'" (Matthew 26:34). Peter didn't believe Him. He knew how much he loved the Lord—he would never deny Jesus. Or so he thought.

Jesus gave Peter the third warning not once, but twice. After their emotionally exhausting last supper together, Jesus and eleven of the disciples went to the Garden of Gethsemane. There, Jesus took Peter, James, and John aside from the others and told them to "pray that you will not fall into temptation" (Luke 22:40). Then He went off by Himself to fight His own battle. Meanwhile, the men closest to Jesus, who should have been the most motivated to pray for Him, promptly fell asleep.

Within the hour, the Lord came back to find them snoozing. All three were asleep, but the Lord rebuked only Peter: "'Simon,' he said to Peter, 'are you asleep? Could you not keep watch for one hour?'" (Mark 14:37). By then Peter was on top of a snowball. Jesus repeated the command: "Watch and pray so that you will not fall into temptation" (Mark 14:38). *Watch. Pay attention. Something big is coming!* Yet when Jesus returned for the third time, He found them asleep again. "Are you still sleeping and resting? Enough!" (Mark 14:41).

In His repeated warnings, Jesus had addressed Peter by his former name, Simon, instead of as Peter, which means *rock*. How did the reference escape Peter? Why wasn't he paying attention? Wouldn't you think he would notice that the Lord was trying to give him a heads-up that a big temptation was coming?

Not only did Peter miss the Lord's warnings to him, but he also failed to recognize that what Jesus had said would happen to Him was coming to pass. Only a few moments after Jesus awakened Peter, Jewish officials arrived with a detachment of Roman soldiers to arrest Jesus. The just-roused Peter promptly chopped off the ear of Malchus, the high priest's servant. What followed—besides a sometimes overlooked but very impressive ear healing—was yet another rebuke for Peter. "No more of this!" Jesus cried (Luke

22:51). "Put your sword away! Shall I not drink the cup the Father has given me?" (John 18:11). In other words: *Look, Peter, I've been trying to tell you, but you haven't been paying attention. Now you're just going to have to step aside.*

It seems that at that point Peter was a tad confused. One moment he passionately wielded a sword on the Lord's behalf, and the next he ran away from Him. Luke tells us that Peter then turned and "followed at a distance" (Luke 22:54).

As Jesus was led off to trial, Peter hung out in the background waiting to see what would happen. He still didn't seem too concerned about all of the warnings Jesus had given him. He appears instead to have been caught up in the moment and carried along by his circumstances. Peter's snowball was headed downhill.

The soldiers took Jesus to the courtyard of the high priest. When Peter got there, he stood outside while another disciple—probably John, who knew the high priest—gained access for them both. As Peter entered, the girl who opened the gate asked Peter a seemingly harmless question: "You are not one of his disciples, are you?" (John 18:17).

Peter's snowball quickly gained momentum. "I am not," he said (John 18:17). Denial number one. Why did Peter deny that he was one of Jesus' disciples? Did he fear that his life was in danger? Possibly. What I really wonder, though, is why, as soon as the words "I am not" were out of his mouth, Peter didn't hear the Lord's warnings ringing in his ears.

That Peter did not hear them is certain, because not long afterwards he denied the Lord again. As he warmed himself at the fire of the Lord's enemies, he talked with the men who had arrested Jesus. When they detected his Galilean accent, they asked him the same question: Was he one of Jesus' disciples? "I am not," he insisted (John 18:25). Another denial. Again, Peter was oblivious to Christ's warnings.

The third denial seems to me the hardest for him to avoid. By this time, Peter had slept through prayer time, impulsively cut off a man's ear, run and hid, lied twice, and had been hanging out with the high priest's servants for well over an hour. By the time the third question came, Peter had gotten in pretty deep. Of course, that's usually how it is. The bigger the snowball, the more difficult it is to manage.

"Didn't I see you with him in the olive grove?" asked a relative of the nearly one-eared Malchus (John 18:26). Peter might have said simply, "I don't know this man you're talking about." But he didn't. Mark tells us that Peter actually "began to call down curses on himself" and swear that he didn't know Jesus (Mark 14:71).

At that moment, the rooster crowed.

Only Luke records what happened next: "The Lord turned and looked straight at Peter" (Luke 22:61). It must have been quite a look because "then Peter remembered the word the Lord had spoken to him: 'Before the rooster crows today, you will disown me three times'" (Luke 22:61). It wasn't even the rooster that finally jogged Peter's memory. It was eye contact with Jesus. What message did the Lord's look convey? Pain? Or love for his foolish, sinful friend? Whatever Peter saw in the Lord's eyes, it convicted him. "And he went outside and wept bitterly" (Luke 22:62). Peter's snowball had crashed.

Peter messed up. Instead of heeding the Lord's warnings, he self-confidently proclaimed his loyalty. Instead of praying, he slept. Instead of staying close to Jesus, he ran away. In short, instead of following Jesus that night, Peter followed his own instincts.

I used to shake my head at Peter and click my tongue—*tsk, tsk*—until I noticed that there were similarities in our stories. In moments of passionate love for Christ, I, too, have felt that I would never deny Him and that I could maybe even die for Him. But then the rubber would meet the road, and I would realize that most of the time I couldn't even live for Him. I know what it feels like to be so physically and emotionally exhausted that prayer seems less important than escaping into sleep. And often when my circumstances have turned overwhelming or confusing, I have justified leaving the Lord's side to try to regroup.

In fact, I have to admit that it is not in Peter's many triumphs that I am most like him, but at his points of failure. Just as I self-confidently relied on what I thought I knew when I was in my teens, Peter self-confidently relied on his own courage and devotion. Peter was indeed a courageous and devoted man, yet his courage turned to fear and his devotion turned to disloyalty just when it mattered most. In our self-confidence, we both thought that *knowing* right from wrong meant that we would automatically choose to do right. Wrong.

Self-confidence sounds like a good thing, but actually, it's a form of pride that makes us forget how much we need the Lord. We must trade our self-reliance for Christ-reliance. We must exchange our haughtiness for humility. Consider the following wisdom from St. Augustine:

An orator was once asked, "What is the first precept in eloquence?"

"Delivery," the orator answered.

"What is the second?"

"Delivery."

"What [is] the third?"

"Delivery."

So, Augustine concluded, if you ask me in regard to the precepts of the Christian religion, I will answer, first, second, and third, "Humility."[1]

Confidence that comes from trusting in Christ's strength, not our own, is an expression of humility. It is only in trusting Jesus that we can hope to avoid failure.

We like to think that warnings of impending failure will keep us from it, but they are not enough. Peter was warned that Satan had plans to sift him, that he needed to pray, and that he would deny Christ. His first two denials could also have served as warnings if he had remembered his Master's words. But all of these warnings weren't enough to keep him from failure.

Like Peter, I had been warned—by my parents, by God's Word, by teachers, and by my previous failures. But the warnings fell on deaf ears because I was determined to rely on myself. Without humility, we do not think we need warnings, so we do not heed them.

I no longer judge Peter. Now his story reminds me that *knowing better* doesn't always mean *doing better*. It reminds me how easy it has been for me to find myself atop a careening snowball. It reminds me what it feels like to fail and then weep bitter tears. But mostly, Peter's story gives me hope, because Peter didn't *remain* a failure. He went on, along with the other apostles, to establish the Christian church. His past didn't negate his future—even though his most public failure came *after* he had put his faith in Christ.

Now when I am tempted to judge myself against the standards of others, or to judge others against mine, I try to remember that our human standards for judging aren't always right. God doesn't compare us to others, but to Himself. When our perspective is the same as God's, we see the scales begin to balance. We see that it doesn't matter who we are or how well we appear to have behaved in life, for we've all missed God's mark. By trusting Him and walking in the power of His Holy Spirit, we are all capable of turning around and living the kind of godly lives that can rock the world.

If you are tempted to judge yourself or others, remember that Jesus loved to teach that things are not always what they seem. What looks black might just be white, and what looks white might just be black. He taught just such a lesson the day the Pharisees brought before Him a woman caught in the act of adultery.

A Stone's Throw Away

She was an adulteress, but more importantly, she was a pawn in the hands of the scribes and Pharisees. These guys were know-it-alls. Unlike I was as a thirteen-year-old, they really *did* know their stuff. One thing they knew was that they wanted to be rid of Jesus. So they orchestrated a battle of wits designed to put Jesus between a rock and a hard place—between the Roman government and the Jewish law.

Jesus sat down in the temple courts to teach. But when the scribes and Pharisees brought before Him a woman caught in the act of adultery, He was suddenly sitting as a judge (see John 8:1–11). Where the woman's partner in crime was, we are not told.

Perhaps the Pharisees allowed him to escape, or maybe he was part of their scheme. Regardless, the woman stood alone in her shame in front of the entire assembly.

Her accusers presented Jesus with a problem they thought He could not solve. In essence they asked Him, "Do we stone her or not? Moses said we should, but Rome says we can't. Who wins?" The Master's response showed not only His wisdom, but also His strength. These men could not rush Him. They could not fluster Him. John said that He "bent down and started to write on the ground with his finger" (John 8:6). When His enemies continued to press Him for an answer, "He straightened up and said to them, 'If any one of you is without sin, let him be the first to throw a stone at her'" (John 8:7).

Suddenly, things were topsy-turvy. The tables had been turned. Instead of being the trapped, Jesus was the trapper. The prosecutors found themselves on the witness stand. The woman in the middle of the assembly was no longer the center of attention. With one sentence, Jesus forced those who had pointed fingers at the woman to point at themselves.

When no one picked up a stone, Jesus again "stooped down and wrote on the ground" (John 8:8). I cannot wait to ask Jesus what He wrote. Whatever it was, it had a profound effect on the woman's accusers. One by one they filed away, no longer willing to condemn her. The scribes and Pharisees were forced to admit publicly that they, too, were sinners. Because of the way Jesus had addressed their question, their admission didn't even require words.

When all her accusers had gone, Jesus released the woman from all condemnation. "Go now," He said, "and leave your life of sin" (John 8:11). His look allowed her to go in peace, with a new lease on life. Jesus had also looked at the scribes and Pharisees, and His look had made them walk away with their heads hung.

I know what it's like to get both looks. Although my sins may be "smaller" today than they used to be, I certainly don't think I know everything, and I'm far from having "arrived." When I betray the Lord, Christ's look at my sins is one of pain. But when I am broken in shame and contrition, His look is one of tenderness and forgiveness.

With every failure, I remember what it feels like to be the shamed center of attention. When I am tempted to judge someone else, I remember the scribes and Pharisees who discovered how pointless it is to throw stones. How about you? Do you read Peter's story and think, *He should have known better*? Do you read the woman's story and thank God that you have never been *that* bad? How about when you hear your neighbor's story? Or when you remember your own? Are you holding a stone?

Jesus was clear: Sin is sin. Peter's story is the woman's story is the Pharisees' story is my story is your story. We all fail. We're all guilty. We all need a lifeline. It's time to drop our stones of condemnation so our hands can toss a lifeline of hope to the hurting, broken people all around us. But first we have to take hold of that lifeline ourselves by dealing with our own guilt.

Part Two

THE
TRUTH

4

A Grief Deserved

Putting Guilt in Perspective

❧ WE ALL deal with guilt at one time or another. We feel guilty for things we've done, things we haven't done; words spoken, words unspoken; acts committed, acts omitted; things we thought we should have done, things we want undone.

Although it's a horrible feeling, guilt serves a useful purpose: It lets us know that, more than anything else in life, we need God's forgiveness. In fact, the need to give and receive forgiveness is a major reason people seek counseling. In *The Freedom and Power of Forgiveness*, John MacArthur says: "The typical counselee's most troublesome problems would be significantly diminished (and in some cases solved completely) by a right understanding of what Scripture says about forgiveness."[1]

Dealing with guilt is one of the lifelines that can pull us from the quicksand of regret. But before we can take hold of that line, we need to put guilt in proper perspective by answering three questions:

- Why are we accountable to God?
- What are His requirements for us?
- Where does our guilt originate?

Once we have the answers to these questions, we can begin to understand the solution that God has provided to the problem of our guilt.

CREATING ACCOUNTABILITY

To understand why we are accountable to God, we literally have to go back to the beginning. "In the beginning God created the heavens and the earth" (Genesis 1:1). God has the right to make the rules that we live by and to hold us accountable to them because He created everything, including us.

By the power of His spoken Word, God created the universe. Although we may not know exactly *how* He did it, we can know that He *did*. In fact, we're responsible to know that He did. All we need to do is look around us to see that Creation was no cosmic accident. The apostle Paul said: "What may be known about God is plain...because God has made it plain.... For since the creation of the world God's invisible qualities—his eternal power and divine nature—have been clearly seen, being understood from what has been made, so that men are without excuse" (Romans 1:19–20). Without excuse for what? For not acknowledging who He is and what He has done.

Skeptics often attempt to use science to refute the truth of Creation, but they have never been able to disprove it, and they never will. If we study the physical laws of the universe or the processes of creation, we will discover God's wisdom in their order. If we try to comprehend the vastness of our universe (a universe that is *still* expanding!), we will understand the immensity of the Creator. If we consider the fact that in a mere handful of soil there are *millions* of tiny living organisms, we will conclude that God is sovereign over every detail of existence. If we look at creatures that delight in their absurdity (ever seen a duck-billed platypus?), we will realize that God has a wonderful sense of humor. If we study the delicate balance and precise equilibrium of our universe— galaxy after galaxy, star after star, planet after planet, all flawlessly suspended—we will know that only God can sustain it moment by moment. Everything in the universe continually testifies to the truth of God's existence. The Creator lives!

I've heard some people say that creation *itself* is God—that He is embodied in the totality of His own work. Yet Solomon said: "The heavens, even the highest heavens, cannot contain him" (2 Chronicles 2:6). How can God *be* creation if creation cannot contain Him? Paul says that, in fact, the opposite is true:

> "The God who made the world and everything in it is the Lord of heaven and earth and does not live in temples built by hands. And he is not served by human hands, as if he needed anything, because he himself gives all men life and breath and everything else.... 'For in him we live and move and have our being.'" (Acts 17:24–25, 28)

God is not in creation; creation is *in Him*. Creation is not a *container for* God; it is an *expression of* God.

And when He had created, "God saw that it was good" (Genesis 1:25). Perfect design. Perfect execution. No mistakes. No regrets. Everywhere and at all times, God's creation reveals the perfection of His character to all who will engage their senses.

See Me in the rainbow arching across the sky
and in the bountiful colors of autumn.
Watch as I paint a purple sunset.
Smell Me in the summer rain, in fields of jasmine,
and in the cedar forests.
Touch Me as you wiggle your toes in the sand,
fall facedown into fresh snow,
or stroke the cheek of a newborn babe.
Hear Me in the waves crashing against the shore,
in the birds of the rain forest,
and the thunder of a thousand hooves on the Serengeti.
Taste Me in the first fruit of summer,
or the ice-cold water of a mountain stream,
or the honey straight from the comb.

Through His creation, God says: "I am; I am here; and I am good."

Although God spoke the universe into existence, He intimately formed mankind. He formed Adam from the dust of the ground, took Eve from Adam's rib, and knit together the rest of us in our mothers' wombs (see Psalm 139). His breath of life is in our lungs (Genesis 2:7). God made us in His image, so in some ways we are like Him. We are moral beings who are able to feel, reason, and choose.

God didn't create the universe or us without purpose. He has revealed Himself in creation and made us in His image so that we might seek and know Him.

> From one man he made every nation of men, that they should inhabit the whole earth; and he determined the times set for them and the exact places where they should live. God did this *so that men would seek him and perhaps reach out for him and find him*, though he is not far from each one of us. (Acts 17:26–27, emphasis added)

From the beginning, God intended to have a relationship with us. He wants us—wants *you*—to know Him. Look in a mirror and ponder the fact that God made you like Himself. Why did He do that? He wants you to see Him in the design of the image that stares back at you. He wants you to look beyond creation to the Creator and to see and praise Him for who He is—powerful, wise, beautiful, perfect, good, and just. He wants you to realize that *creation is* because *He is* and that because He made it, *He owns it*. "Everything under heaven belongs to me" (Job 41:11). That includes you.

THE PERFECT REQUIREMENT

God created, so God has the right to set the rules and to hold us accountable to them. What are God's requirements? Since He created a perfect universe, that's what He demands—perfection. Anything that doesn't meet that standard is sin.

Sin. We like to disassociate ourselves from that word. It's something other people deal with, not us. Many people are con-fused about it. Some believe that the word describes only "really bad" acts such as murder or child abuse. Others use it to describe only those things that trespass boundaries set by themselves or society. Some even attach the label of sin to such delights as—hold on, this will be hard to take—*chocolate!* Chocolate, a sin? I shudder at the thought.

So what is the standard? Where is the marker? How do we know when have we crossed the line into sin?

Jesus said, "Be perfect, therefore, as your heavenly Father is perfect" (Matthew 5:48). Pure motives. Flawless obedience. Perfect love. Every second of every minute of every day of your life. *That's* the standard. If we fail to meet it, we have crossed the line into sin. In order to avoid God's condemnation, we must be perfectly spot-less before Him.

That's where guilt comes in. We *feel* guilty because we *are* guilty. We are guilty because a perfect God created perfect things to exist within the boundaries of perfect laws. You and I are not perfect. We have broken the laws of perfection that were written on our hearts by the Divine Legislator. Our sin violates our innate sense of what is good and right and holy. The result is guilt—a grief deserved.

But if the universe was created perfect, how did we become sinful? If "it is good," then why aren't we? To answer this question we again have to go back to the beginning.

ORIGINAL SIN, ORIGINAL GUILT

God created mankind good, but we didn't stay that way.

Though God made man in His image, there were certain parts

of His character that He reserved only for Himself. For instance, we are not omniscient, omnipotent, sovereign—or immutable. God is *immutably* good. He never changes. He's not even capable of change. Unlike Him, we are susceptible to changing from good to bad. A. W. Pink puts it this way: "Herein we may perceive the infinite distance which separates the highest creature from the Creator. Creaturehood and mutability are correlative terms. If the creature was not mutable by nature, it would not be a creature; it would be God."[2]

It was therefore not a given that Adam and Eve would remain perfect. One day in the Garden they made a choice that changed them, and when they changed, so did we. God had not given them many rules to follow—just one, in fact. They were forbidden to eat from a certain tree in the Garden of Eden. But they chose to do it anyway, and God had to respond to their disobedience.

THE VERDICT

Romans 11:22 says, "Behold then the kindness and severity of God" (NASB). God is both completely kind and completely uncompromising. To think of Him as only one or the other will lead us to fairy-tale thinking. He will either seem like a jolly Santa Claus who winks at our sin and continues to bestow gifts on us, or like a fire-breathing dragon who tramples anyone who dares approach Him. Before we can appreciate God's kindness, we need to understand His uncompromising nature when it comes to sin.

When Adam and Eve sinned, God didn't say, "Oh, that's okay; nobody's perfect." Instead, He pronounced His judgment. Childbearing and gardening haven't been the same since (see Genesis 3). A quick read through Genesis doesn't reveal all the consequences of the sin in the Garden. The list is mind-boggling.

Adam and Eve went from being the crown of God's creation to outcasts from His garden paradise. Just as their physical labor increased after the Fall, so did their mental and emotional labor. No longer could they choose to be good, as God had created them, for they had become slaves to their own corrupt desires. Their minds, which had been unobstructed by bias or depravity, became subject to conflicting thoughts and emotions. In *A Grief Observed*, C. S. Lewis described this struggle in his own mind:

> Five senses; an incurably abstract intellect; a haphazardly selective memory; a set of preconceptions and assumptions so numerous that I can never examine more than a minority of them—never become even conscious of them all. How much of total reality can such an apparatus let through?[3]

After Adam and Eve's sin, nothing would come easily—except sin. That would come all too easily, for the choice they made had been an all-or-nothing venture. Unhindered intimacy with God was lost, right along with unhampered obedience.

God's judgment fell on Adam's progeny as well. I like the way R. C. Sproul paraphrases St. Augustine's view on the matter: "All men were seminally in Adam when he was condemned. Those that were 'in Adam' were subsequently punished with him."[4] Adam represented all of us, so when he fell, we all fell. When Adam sinned, God imputed his guilt to all who would come after him.

In other words, not only are you guilty for the sins you have committed in your life, you were guilty from the day you were born. King David understood that: "Surely I was sinful at birth, sinful from the time my mother conceived me" (Psalm 51:5). Before you felt regret for your own sins, you suffered for the sins of another. Because of that sin, Adam's consequences are ours, including the worst judgment of all, death—physical and spiritual. God said to Adam, "You will surely die" (Genesis 2:17), and God tells us that apart from Him we are "dead in [our] transgressions and sins" (Ephesians 2:1).

Like Adam, we suffer consequences for our choices and the sorrow of knowing that we have been cast away from the presence of God. We not only suffer from guilt and regret for our own sin, but we feel the wrath of a holy God against the sinful *nature* that we inherited. Oh, not that we sit around munching on Cap'n Crunch, thinking, *Wow, is my nature depraved*. But when we think about it—really dwell on it in light of Scripture—that's the conclusion we must face. Adam fell, and from that time forward, we have all been born to die.

Behold the severity of God.

SEEKING JUSTICE

God loves us, but our sin is detestable to Him, and His holiness and justice demand payment for it. Before we can have a right relationship with Him, the price for our sin must be paid.

Recently, I asked a friend if he thought that he had a clean soul. His reply was not uncommon: "My soul is clean because I'm a good person, and I try never to hurt anyone. And when I have messed up, boy, have I made up for it by suffering royally." My friend's first misconception is that he is clean because he *intends* to be clean.

Since he doesn't *try* to hurt anyone, he figures that when he does, it doesn't count. What he has failed to understand is the requirement God has placed on him and his profound inability to meet that requirement. God doesn't judge us by our intentions.

Unfortunately for my friend, his second perception is also wrong: We cannot excuse ourselves or suffer our way out of sin and guilt, though many people try. They try to "work off" the penalty of sin by some means—even if they're not consciously aware of what they're trying to do. Here are three of the most common ways people try to do this:

- *By suffering.* Like my friend, we sometimes believe that God forgives our sin because we suffer pain. Often we believe that being afflicted with the consequences of our sin is punishment enough. Other times we believe that suffering that is unrelated to our sin will cancel our debt. These perceptions are wrong. We would have to suffer an eternity to pay the debt of our sin.

- *By self-punishment.* Some people physically beat themselves as punishment for their sin. Others simply beat themselves up verbally or mentally. But punishing ourselves only ensures that we feel more pain and more defeat. It certainly doesn't impress God.

- *By being a "good person."* It seems logical that if we can bring on God's condemnation by doing something bad, then we should be able to earn His pleasure by doing something good. But Isaiah 64:6 says, "All our righteous acts are like filthy rags." When we are apart from God, He doesn't consider anything we do to be "good," and He actually despises our efforts to please Him. It is only *after* we have been reconciled to Him that He considers anything we do to be good.

We have severed our relationship with God, and nothing we can do on our own will take us one step back to Him. Not one of our good deeds will make us right with God.

God still loves us and wants to have a relationship with us, but our sin gets in the way. It gets in God's way because His justice must be satisfied, and it gets in our way because it will not allow us to accept His love. At heart, we, too, desire justice. We would love to skip the punishment and consequences of sin, of course, but deep down we know that we are guilty, and until our guilt is taken care of, we continually ask ourselves, *How could God love me after what I've done?* Without a remedy for our guilt, we dismiss God's love as a nice idea.

So it is our guilt that tells us not only that we have severed our relationship with God, but that we have exposed ourselves to His wrath. We were born condemned, helpless in our sin, and apart from God we are helpless to do anything about it.

THE POINT OF GRACE

Doomed by a man in a garden simply because we are related to him? Not fair, you say? If we are born with a propensity to sin, why does God then condemn us for sinning? There are many who cry "not fair" and refuse to believe in or love a God who would condemn all of mankind for the sin of one man. The fairness question is a valid one—but God gave us the answer to it on the first Christmas morning.

Actually, He had given the answer nine months earlier, when the Virgin Mary conceived a child. Why is that so important? Because the fact that Mary was a virgin meant that not only was Joseph not the father, but that, more importantly, neither was Adam. There was no bad seed, as it were—no Garden consequences. No imputed guilt was passed on to the child, and Jesus was born with the potential to live a perfect life. That's huge. If it was again possible for a man to be perfect, then it was also possible for him to retain his relationship with God and not be subject to judgment or death.

So it was for Jesus. He eluded the curse that God had placed on mankind because he was the Son of God, or as John calls Him, "the Word" (John 1:1). The Word who had been with God eternally came to earth disguised as a baby in a manger—the Almighty with skin. As Max Lucado marvels: "God as a fetus. Holiness sleeping in a womb. The creator of life being created. God was given eyebrows, elbows, two kidneys, and a spleen. He stretched against the walls and floated in the amniotic fluids of his mother. God had come near."[5]

God made Himself into our image to live the perfect life that we couldn't. Just as He had through creation, God said in Jesus, "I am here."

> *See Me growing up in Nazareth,*
> *playing in the dirt that I created.*
> *Listen as I teach the teachers of Israel*
> *and amaze them with My understanding.*
> *Watch the face of the wedding host when*
> *he tastes the water that I've turned into wine.*
> *Laugh as I take a stroll with My friend…on a nearby lake.*
> *Watch as I tell the wind and waves to hush—and they do.*

I am here.
Listen as I tell My friend Lazarus to come out of a tomb,
not long before I say good-bye to My mother and enter one.

The incarnation—God becoming man—is hardly fathomable. Yet it is the mysterious truth that, when embraced, explains other mysteries. "The more you think about it, the more staggering it gets," J. I. Packer once said. " Nothing in fiction is so fantastic as is the truth of the incarnation...but it makes sense of everything else that the New Testament contains."[6]

In the Old Testament, God sent His prophets to speak His Word and give light to men, and repeatedly the prophets, and God's Word, were rejected. A read through the Old Testament is like reading a continual plea from heaven, "Listen to me, listen to me, listen to me." But God's pleas were ignored. So God responded with four hundred years of silence—and then one resounding Word.

Jesus.

Everything God wants to say to us can be found in the life of Jesus.

I made you; therefore, I love you.
You blew it; therefore, I cursed you.
I still love you; therefore,
watch as I take Myself and you to the only place
where My love and My justice meet—
to the cross, to the point of My grace.

The cross—that mysterious and incomprehensible place where man punishes God for nothing, and God punishes Himself for everything. At the cross, man again rejected God's Word, but this time our rejecting Him made it possible for Him to accept us. God ordained His own rejection for our sake.

Jesus Christ, the only one who lived a perfect life and didn't deserve God's just punishment, deliberately took that punishment in a death-by-proxy for us. Jesus, like Adam, represented mankind. He avoided Adam's curse in birth to *become* Adam's curse in death. He was no different from us in that He was born to die. But He was very different from us in that He didn't have to. God's justice imputed Adam's guilt to us. God's love imputed our guilt to Himself. We suffer for the sins of another and cry "unfair" only to have our cries silenced by one glimpse of God on a tree—unfairly suffering for our sins.

God's Word hung on the cross until He spoke His final word: "Finished." His work, which reached from creation to redemption, was complete. God's laws of perfection were fulfilled in Christ's life, and His laws of love were fulfilled in His death. God's law condemns us, but His love saves us. Who else but God could find a place where His purity could meet our depravity? Max Lucado says it profoundly: "Never did the obscene come so close to the holy as it did on Calvary."[7]

Was the death of one man enough to satisfy God's judgment against the many? God had condemned us for the sin of one; would He then save us for the death of One? Because Jesus met God's requirement for perfection, His death was enough. Justice was served, and the Father was satisfied. The Son was raised from the dead, taken into heaven, and seated at the Father's right hand. "He, having offered one sacrifice for sins for all time, sat down at the right hand of God" (Hebrews 10:12, NASB).

Many of us have heard repeatedly about how amazing grace is—how wonderful it is that God's favor shines on us although we've done nothing to deserve it. The more deeply we contemplate God's holiness and our sinfulness, the more astonishing it seems. We can reconcile God's grace toward us only in light of His love, and we can reconcile His love for us only in light of His grace. It truly *is* amazing.

Jesus has paid the price for guilt-ridden, regretful people. He met God's requirement on our behalf and made it possible to abolish guilt. All we need do is sincerely confess and repent of our sin and receive God's forgiveness. It is *finished.* Jesus is now going about the business of living.

Shouldn't we be, too?

5

The No-Condemnation Clause

Opting out of Guilt

🌿 WE NEED to get rid of our guilt. Without resolution, it can spawn a myriad of problems—among them the persistent, debilitating feeling of regret.

We have seen where healthy guilt originates: God requires that we be perfect, but after Adam chose not to be, we as his offspring couldn't be. We are by nature sinful. God in His mercy, however, has provided us a way out of our guilt.

Scripture reveals that since the beginning of time, God has entered into covenants with men. Some of these covenants have been with all mankind, some with nations, and some with individuals. Often, God has given the other parties to the contract something unconditionally; that is, He has not required them do anything to receive the promised blessing. Sometimes, however, God has stipulated that He will not fulfill His part of the contract unless the other parties fulfill theirs. This was the kind of covenant that God made with His chosen people through Moses at Mt. Sinai. The Israelites would receive the blessings of the covenant only if they obeyed God's laws perfectly (see Exodus 19:5–6).

God, who is always true to His word, remained faithful to this covenant. The Israelites acknowledged the contract, accepted its terms, and then consistently failed to keep their end of the bargain.

THE OPTIONS

When God entered into this agreement with the Israelites, He did so knowing that they would not be able to fulfill the law. He used the covenant to show them—and us—that it is impossible for mankind to meet His standards. Because we are powerless to keep it, the law shows us our sinfulness and helps us realize our need for a Savior. As Galatians 3:24 says, "So the law was put in charge to lead us to Christ."

The penalties for not keeping the law would be irrevocable were it not for the fact that God has created a new covenant through the death of His Son. Imagine God saying something like this:

I know that you're in trouble. In fact, I saw this coming,
and I sent my Son to straighten things out.
I have some good news for you:
My Son fulfilled the old contract for you.
I'm now willing to toss out the old agreement
and make a new one with you—

in fact, it's already signed with His blood.
He's looking for you right now to tell you about it,
and are you going to love it!
He's going to tell you that He paid your penalty on that old deal.
Now there's only one thing you must do,
because there's only one stipulation in the new contract.
You must believe Him. Your faith is your signature.

Because Jesus was the only person ever to fulfill all of God's requirements, He was the only one who could negotiate a new deal for us. In God's eyes, we also can become perfect—not by *doing,* but by *believing* in what Christ has done. "Clearly no one is justified before God by the law, because 'The righteous will live by faith'" (Galatians 3:11). This was God's plan all along. The old deal was meant to point us to our need for the new deal, which requires only our faith as our signature.

Some people cannot accept this truth. I guess it must seem too easy, because they keep trying to make the old deal work. Many try to earn their way into God's good graces, although they might not even realize that that's what they're doing. Probably not many people reading this book would say that they put any stock in Buddhism or Hinduism, but what about "do-goodism"? They think, *Maybe I can do enough good things and avoid enough bad things to earn my way into heaven.* How many of us, if we are being honest, would have to admit that we're hoping God will somehow grant us "time off for good behavior"? If God is loving and good, surely He'll let us go to heaven—right?

The fact is that there is only one place where God's love and justice converge. There is only *one* point of grace and *one* person through whom we can be freed from our guilt and thereby have a relationship with the Father. That point is the cross, and that person is Jesus.

The bad news is that we have destroyed ourselves with our sin. The good news is that God offers us new birth through His Son. But to enter into that new birth takes faith. To be freed from Adam's legacy of guilt, we must escape his lineage. We must trade Adam's seed for the seed of Christ. We must be born again and have God as our Father.

Fantastic as it must seem, all it takes to be born again is to believe that Christ lived a perfect life, died a sacrificial death to pay the price for our sin, and rose from the dead, or as the apostle Paul stated it, "that Christ died for our sins according to the Scriptures, that he was buried, that he was raised on the third day according to the Scriptures..." (1 Corinthians 15:3–4). Believing this good news puts your signature on the covenant that God offers you through Christ and frees you from guilt.

So guilt is a good thing in that it leads us to Christ for forgiveness. But feeling guilty can also be a bad thing. Once we've confessed, repented, and asked for God's forgiveness, any lingering feelings of guilt are just that—feelings. We not only need to *be* forgiven, but we also need to *feel* forgiven.

If we have received Christ and God has removed our guilt, but we still feel guilty, the answer is the same. Once we get right with God, it is *by faith* that we are pronounced "not guilty." In other words, we must *believe* that because of Christ we are not guilty. When we believe that, we can overcome regret and go about the business of living.

Faith isn't just a nice thought, something we inherit from our parents, or a product of our upbringing. Faith is an *act;* it is something we *do.* It is the decision and act of placing our trust completely in Jesus. It is trusting that all our sins—every character flaw and every thought, word, and deed that causes us regret—have been punished on Calvary and no longer hold any power in our life. Faith may sound simple, but it is profound. In fact, although the redemption we receive is free, our faith will demand everything from us.

SORRY FOR WHAT?

Our faith leads us to *repentance,* and repentance leads to freedom from regret. If we haven't changed the thing that is causing our regret, then we cannot stop regretting—even if we believe we are forgiven.

A wise Bible teacher taught me that repentance consists of four elements: conviction, confession, contrition, and conversion.

Conviction is simply being convinced that we are wrong. This can be painful—especially when we sin after salvation or when we feel we should have "known better." There is a special pain we feel when our actions have brought shame on the name of Christ or have caused unbelievers or new Christians to stumble.

Confession is acknowledging *and* declaring our sin. We are always to confess our sin to God. But sometimes it is also necessary to confess to other people. Do not confuse confession with admission. Confession means to agree with *God's perspective* about our sin.

Contrition is being sorry for the pain we've caused. Sorrow for the pain we've caused others and ourselves makes us compassionate. But it is the deeper sorrow for causing *God* pain that changes the very core of our character. King David said, "For I know my transgressions, and my sin is always before me. Against you, you only, have I sinned and done what is evil in your sight, so that you are proved right when you speak and justified when you judge" (Psalm 51:3–4). David's words reveal a contrite heart, and that's where spiritual growth happens.

Genesis 25 shows us the kind of contrition that falls short. Esau despised his birthright, which was a gift from God. In a moment of passion and hunger, Esau revealed his true feelings toward God when he sold his birthright to his twin brother, Jacob. Esau eventually regretted his move, but instead of regretting the sin of despising his birthright, he regretted only the consequence of losing his blessing. If we are sorry merely for the consequences of our wrong actions, then we have come only as far as Esau, who regretted his loss but not his sin.

Finally, *conversion* is the act of changing what we are currently doing into what we should be doing. If we are truly repentant, we will experience three things: *gratitude* for the knowledge that we have sinned against God and that He forgives us our transgressions; *humility* because that forgiveness came with a big price tag; and *change* as we are transformed more and more into the likeness of Christ. If we gratefully and humbly remember that God forgives us and that our sins were nailed to the cross with His Son, there is hope that we will complete our repentance by changing and turning from our sin.

So the questions are these: What *are* you sorry for? Are you sorry for your crimes, or merely for their consequences? Are you sorry for the pain you have caused God and other people, or simply for the fact that you feel regret? Have you placed your trust completely and only in Jesus Christ, or is your pride fooling you with the subtle excuses we sometimes use to justify ourselves? ("Well, I didn't know any better. I was young" or "It's all her fault" or "It's all Satan's fault" or even "It's all God's fault for not equipping me.") We can cleanse our conscience of guilt only when we are sorry for the right things.

FROM REGRET TO REVIVAL

Although salvation is a one-time event, repentance begins when we put our faith in Christ and continues for as long as we battle with sin—which will be throughout our earthly lives. Without complete repentance, it's impossible to let go of guilt or regret because we can't let go of them if we don't let go of sin.

What if we become trapped by sin and don't feel the need to repent, don't want to repent, or feel we can't repent? Then we need to cry out for *revival*. Revival is the reawakening of our souls by the Holy Spirit. When sin has snared us and turned us from repentance, praying for revival is the only way we can get rid of guilt. When our souls are revived—made aware of their need and desire for God—we will experience a rekindled longing to change and be cleansed. Then, and only then, is repentance possible.

Two things will cause us to cry out for revival: an awareness of our sin and the memory of our once passionate love for Jesus. As Charles Spurgeon wrote:

> The true believer, when he is confronted with his need for revival, will long for it. He will not be happy, but will at once begin to strain after it. The true believer will pray day and night, "O Lord, revive thy work!" And what will make

that true Christian groan for revival? When he reflects on what Christ has done for him...when he hears someone tell a story about a fellow believer who is experiencing great joy in the Lord...when he attends a lively fellowship and feels no emotion in his heart, he will groan for his own revival.[1]

If we are willing, revival will give us the strength to turn away from any sin—even when we know that to do so will mean suffering consequences. Repenting because of our faith, knowing that suffering will follow, is an indication of revival. And as Spurgeon was quick to point out, that is God's work, not ours:

> Make no resolutions as to what you will do; your resolutions will surely be broken as they are made.... I urge you: do nothing until you have first prayed to God, crying out, "O Lord, revive thy work." Begin, then, by humbling yourself—giving up all hope of reviving yourself, but beginning at once with the firm prayer and earnest supplication to God: "O Lord, what I cannot, you do for me. O Lord, revive thy work!"[2]

Repentance is the outward act of inward change—and inward change comes only from the work of the Holy Spirit. Within ourselves we can't invoke sufficient passion or faith in Christ to repent. It is wholly a work of God. I know firsthand that the answer to a broken spirit is not found in yet another resolution to "do better." Through the years, my journals have become full of entries such as the following:

> I have been, and indeed am, so far away. It's been horrible. Lonely. It feels like tonight that I may have taken my first

step back toward the Lord. I've learned nothing is a given, though. A sincere prayer and a cleansing cry do not repentance and revival make. Oh, for revival! That is my prayer. Indeed the only important prayer I can utter right now. Without that, all other requests or praises are hollow and vain.

We don't clean ourselves up for God; rather, He reaches down into the pit where we are and lifts us out. All we can do is groan and pray for God to come in and change us and be willing to be made willing. Only then do we have any hope of revival and repentance.

There is no one more miserable than the one who is convicted, even contrite, but has not changed. Without complete repentance, misery ensues. Many Christians, even mature ones, find themselves in this place—trapped by a sin from which they can't seem to escape and shocked that they were trapped in the first place.

The same teacher who taught me about repentance repeated this phrase often: "Don't ever be surprised at your ability to sin!" Max Lucado puts it in even stronger terms: "Given the right lure, at the right moment, aimed at the right weakness, there is not a person alive who wouldn't pull back the curtain and live out his vilest fantasy."[3]

Pulling back the curtain only to be tapped on the shoulder by the Lord is indeed painful. But if you are convicted of sin and do not turn away from it, you are probably suffering something even worse. Dr. James Dobson describes the struggle:

Even when we ignore its condemnation, the conscience is a formidable opponent of irresponsibility and it will not

permit gross violations of moral laws without a struggle....
People [who ignore their conviction and persist in sin] can
be some of the most miserable men and women on the
face of the earth. Their behavior has contradicted their personal code of ethics and all attempts to reconcile the two
have been futile."[4]

To be divided against ourselves brings a unique and excruciat-
ing anguish, a pain that most people cannot live with for long without paying a terrible price—spiritually, emotionally, and perhaps
even physically.

Often we wait for our snowball to crash before we become willing to confess and repent. We wait for consequences to chase us
down and make us even more miserable before we will change.

But sometimes it is God *sparing us* from such pain that drives
us to repent. The Bible is replete with stories of God's patience and
generosity toward men *while* they were sinning. Paul said, "God's
kindness is meant to lead you to repentance" (Romans 2:4, PHP).

Aren't we this way with our own children? Don't we give to
them, hoping they will respond in gratitude and obedience? How
much more does our heavenly Father give us! How sad that too
often we interpret His continued generosity toward us not as for-
bearance, but as permissiveness. The reason for God's patience is
that we might contrast our shame with His glory and then turn
back to Him. He loves us and wants us to love Him. He longs for
us to desire Him more than we desire the thing that is giving us
temporary pleasure.

Although change can be painful, in the end the reward is great.
Nothing on earth satisfies like a vibrant relationship with the Lord.

If you don't have a relationship like that, don't you think it's time to pursue it? We can do this by expressing faith, humbling our hearts, and returning to Him. "The LORD is good to those whose hope is in him, to the one who seeks him; it is good to wait quietly for the salvation of the LORD" (Lamentations 3:25–26). "Return, O Israel, to the LORD your God. Your sins have been your downfall! Take words with you and return to the LORD" (Hosea 14:1–2).

BEAUTY FOR ASHES

As I have said, guilt and grief over sin are not necessarily bad things. We can appreciate the beauty of the cross only after we contemplate the depth of our sin. Go ahead, mourn your sin; in fact, feel free to wallow in grief for a while. *But don't stop there.* God doesn't intend for us to stay in that place of brokenness. Guilt over our sin is resolved by the wonderful grace of Jesus Christ. I know because I've gone to the cross a broken sinner many times over.

Once we know Jesus as the compassionate healer and wise teacher He was here on earth, it's hard to imagine anyone thinking that He deserved to be cruelly executed on a Roman cross. But once we know Him as Lord and Savior—our best friend, counselor, confidant, and faithful helper—the injustice He endured is more than hard to imagine; it's hard to stomach. Nevertheless, sometimes I make myself go there—to Golgotha.

When I have guilt that I cannot shake, I go there in my mind and imagine the taunts, the murmuring, the crying women, and the soldiers gambling just inches from His pierced feet. I imagine Jesus hanging there in twisted suspension—naked, bruised, swollen, bleeding—laboring for each precious breath. I imagine myself sitting there, at the foot of the cross, eye level with His feet, and I feel the sorrow wash over me.

I think about the fact that I am the one who put Him there. Part of me wants to call Him down, to spare Him such agony. Then I remember that He is *willingly* paying the price for the guilt that is weighing me down. My guilt is no surprise to the Lord. He knew all of it—past, present, and future—before He made the decision to die for it. No, I haven't shocked Him with my sin.

Thank God.

Thank God that He is bigger than my biggest sin and stronger than my worst enemy. Thank God that He uses my failure and guilt to remind me that without Him I am lost—utterly and completely lost. And thank God that He takes me to an empty tomb to remind me that I once was lost, but now I am found.

There was a time, though, when revisiting the cross didn't help me. I wasn't struggling with guilt over my *sin;* instead, I regretted that I had messed up God's plan for my life. My life was supposed to have gone a certain way, so I felt as if my mistakes had ruined it. How could I forgive myself for undermining God's intent for my life? I thought that I would always feel anger and remorse. Only after a long process of healing and restoration—which I describe in the chapters to come—was I able to overcome my regret once and for all.

Some time ago I heard part of an interview with the late musician Rich Mullins. Though I don't remember his exact words, I will never forget the truth he imparted. He said that from the moment we believe in Christ, everything changes. We receive a new biography. We go from being paupers to being royalty. Our problem is that *we don't know it*. Mullins said that while we live here on earth, it is the Holy Spirit's job, through our failures and subsequent restoration, to teach us who we are in Christ. Most of us don't have a clue about the riches that are ours, so we continue living like paupers.

How true that is. We get so caught up in the ugliness of life that we forget who we really are—children of the King of heaven and earth.

When God created man, He made beauty from dust. He breathed His own breath into our lungs and declared, "It is good." We will do well to remember that at salvation God doesn't *fix* us, He *recreates* us. He takes the debris of our broken lives and in some mysterious way begins shaping it into something beautiful. In Christ we are created again. God looks at us and says, "It is *finished*. Therefore, *you* are good."

Amazing grace, indeed.

6

Untold Grief

Secret Sin, Private Pain, Hidden Regret

🌿 WE WERE in my study making our confessions to each other. She had screwed up at work; I had screwed up my finances. The moment was by divine appointment.

Eight months earlier, God had prompted me to talk to my friend Debra, a CPA. I had made a bad financial decision and loaned a substantial amount of money to someone who couldn't pay it back. That decision cost me dearly. I desperately needed to talk to an advisor, but I was too proud. I didn't want to look bad. So for months I avoided talking about the problem. I thought that if I could juggle things a bit and bear the anxiety, it might not be necessary to reveal my problem to anyone. But I learned that persisting in my pride had a price: I suffered increasing insecurity and eight additional months of messed-up finances.

Then one day Debra called and asked me to baby-sit her son the following morning. I understood her need and agreed to help. That same afternoon I was hit with another financial crisis, and I remembered my conviction that I should talk to Debra. Since I normally speak to her only a few times a year, the timing of her call was not lost on me. But frankly I was still resistant, and so the wrestling match with God began. The Lord and I hit the mat, or in this case, my bedroom floor.

Do I really have to tell her, Father?

His Word flooded my mind: "Everyone who does evil hates the light, and will not come into the light for fear that his deeds will be exposed" (John 3:20).

Yes, Lord, I am wrong. My pride makes me afraid of being exposed. What will Debra think of me?

His answer was soft, but still hard to swallow: "Whoever lives by the truth comes into the light" (John 3:21).

Yes, Lord, I understand. I am content to die with the truth. I see that You want me to learn to live by it.

Ding! The wrestling match was over.

Okay, Father, I'll call Debra back and ask her to come early for coffee. If she says yes, I'll talk to her. Obviously, I still wanted to give God every chance to change His mind.

My hope for a reversal of His decision was dashed when Debra said, "Coffee? I'd love to. In fact, I could use a friend right now. I've messed up, and I need to talk to somebody."

In my study the next morning, the truth finally spilled out. I told Debra about my mismanagement and confessed that I had been too proud to seek help. I was relieved when she was comforting and not condemning. Then the tables turned, and Debra revealed her secret. She was also struggling with money, though not her own. She thought that she had failed to file a critical tax form for one of her clients. If so, the oversight would cost her client a lot of money. She was despairing.

She looked at me and said, "How could I have been so dumb? God has blessed me with this business, and now I feel I've let Him down." But Debra hadn't disobeyed God. If she had indeed failed to file the tax form, it wasn't a sin—it was an error. I listened to her and then helped her see that she hadn't disappointed God any more than a toddler disappoints his parents by falling down.

Debra had known it would help if she talked this over with someone, but she was in a quandary about whom to tell. She was single and didn't have the convenience of a live-in confidant. She was reticent about telling her friends, family, or church friends because most of them were also her clients. Telling them could mean that she might have more than her recent failing to consider; she might have a failing business.

I had a similar problem. When you use the words *widow, children,* and *freelance* in the same sentence, your friends and family have more than the usual concern about your finances. To confide in them about my poor decision would have created even more unease and caused them a great deal of worry. I didn't want to deal with that. I also wanted to be sure I confided in someone who was trustworthy.

Thankfully, God had set up an appointment for us. That day in my study the Great Physician began healing both of us as we doctored each other's ills. Debra gave me a prescription for financial recovery; I helped allay her feelings of guilt and regret.

SECURE CELLS

Before we talked, Debra and I both had financial problems. She wisely shared her burden and sought encouragement, accountability, prayer, and advice. But I had compounded my problems because my pride hadn't let me talk about them when I needed to. Instead, I had taken them with me into a prison cell labeled "Secret" and locked the door behind me for eight months.

Being shackled in secrecy created new troubles. I became isolated and severely limited. Because of the lack of communication, I remained defeated and unable to solve my problem. The pain this was causing also remained private. A burden I wished would whither away grew larger instead. An entry I made in my journal at the time reveals another difficulty:

> I'm not concerned about anything anymore because I'm so focused on what's happening with me personally. I have my own internal and external secret crisis going on that I must contend with. It leaves little time or energy for anything or anyone else. Seems secrets breed selfishness along with other problems.

I began to realize that silence and seclusion were neither the solution to my predicament nor the way out of the pain that my pride was causing me. When we do not confess our sins, when we keep our pain private, and when we keep our inevitable regrets to ourselves, we bear a lot of unnecessary grief.

That was King David's experience. He learned that hiding sin can literally make people ill:

When I kept silent, my bones wasted away through my groaning all day long. For day and night your hand was heavy upon me; my strength was sapped as in the heat of summer. (Psalm 32:3–4)

When did David experience this sickening feeling? Possibly after he had tasted the forbidden fruit of adultery and it soured in his stomach. Or maybe it was later, after he attempted to cover the first sin by committing a second one. Keeping sins secret and concealing their consequences can lead to unending regret. And unspoken regret can lead to unspeakable pain.

When Bathsheba's pregnancy was about to expose David's adultery, he resorted to deception. He planned to make it appear that Bathsheba's husband was the father of the child (2 Samuel 11:6–13). He thought that if he could juggle things a bit and bear the anxiety, he wouldn't be exposed. David's plan failed, but he still did not reveal his sin. Instead, he pressed back further into his prison by continuing to conceal the truth. Finally, he had Bathsheba's husband, Uriah, killed (2 Samuel 11:14–17). The secret would never come out. Or so David thought.

I, too, have uttered that word *never* with the intention of concealing sin. I remember one situation years ago, when I was sixteen and in a jam.

I had sinned, and I wanted to hide it. (The prison door opened.)

So I told a lie. (I stepped inside.) It seemed the easiest and least hurtful way of solving my problem. (Just a little juggling, just a little anxiety....) I remember thinking, *One lie to one person and—voilà!—I will be out of this jam.* But then the lie, which was meant for only one person, was spread to most of my family and friends. Now I was in a crisis. I had to either dispel the myth or retell the lie—over and over and over.

So I perpetuated the lie. (I pulled the door shut and locked myself in.) I told myself that I would never reveal the truth. Never! And for years I didn't—not even when I saw the pain the lie was causing and the damage it was doing.

It was not until I confessed my sin that I finally broke free from my prison cell of isolation and pain. My journal entries described my growing oppression…and my agony:

> I am still struggling with a difficult decision. Making public confession seems an unbearable task, even unthinkable. I feel God calling me to it, yet I dread it. The dread is almost tangible. The pain and fear are intense. To remain silent is frustrating, but not so frightening. I want to obey, but my fear is screaming so loudly that I even doubt I hear God's whisper, calling me to confession.
>
> Secrets are prisons. Prisons are painful. Escape is arduous.

REVEALING GRACE

Hiding our true selves when we sin has been our instinct ever since Adam and Eve treated themselves to the forbidden fruit, sewed fig leaves together, and hid from God. We're quite proficient at pretending. We conceal our pain with pious faces and cloak ourselves with righteous behavior, hoping no one will see the darkness in our souls. But it's only when we stand totally naked and exposed before God that we realize that He can face our darkness and not shy away from us. God's love is not blind. He sees us as we are, then covers us with mercy and wraps us in forgiveness. That is the beauty of grace.

Only God's grace can bring us spiritual healing and into fellowship with Him, but grace that isn't revealed cannot be received. How can we accept a gift if we do not know that it exists? We make a way for God to reveal His forgiving grace when we lay our failures before Him.

This is also true with people. Others cannot extend grace to us if we don't give them an opportunity by being vulnerable and open about our shortcomings. Experiencing grace from others is critical for emotional healing and sustaining healthy relationships.

We also need each other for counsel and encouragement. "Woe to one who is alone and falls and does not have another to help" (Ecclesiastes 4:10, NRSV). Some sins, some pain, and some regret cannot be fully resolved without help from the body of Christ. In their book, *Boundaries,* Dr. Henry Cloud and Dr. John Townsend observe what happens to their patients who retreat into seclusion to work out their difficulties:

> They'll spend several hours or a day doing everything possible to get back under control. They'll talk positively to themselves or read Scriptures compulsively to try to make themselves "feel better."
>
> It is only when this attempt at a solution breaks down that they finally realize that these spiritual pains and burdens need to be brought out of themselves to the body of Christ.

To the isolated person, nothing feels more frightening, unsafe, or unwise.[1]

Making the decision to reveal the truth is a battle. No one likes feeling exposed or vulnerable. It is much safer to maintain the status quo by living in our cell. There we feel secure. No one sees us clearly. We may not gain new ground, but we won't get blown away either. Divulging our weaknesses is a dangerous, risky business. It may take all of our courage, cost us our pride, and maybe even cause us some pain.

However, our honesty costs Satan more than it does us. He is the loser in this battle. When we live in the light of authenticity, we live closer to God. We gain strength, grow bolder, and live freer. The enemy cannot stand that light. The truth sends him running for cover—away from us.

To confess is to live dangerously. No walls hide us. No bars keep us confined. Anything is possible. Yet when we are transparent, our prison cells burst open. Problems can be resolved, pain remedied, and a large measure of regret released.

COURAGEOUS CONFESSION

Confession did not come easily for David. He waited a long time. Not that David was comfortable in his sin; in fact, Psalm 51 makes it clear that he was miserable. But he was still clinging to his secret, so God stirred him up. He sent Nathan, a prophet, to rebuke him, and this time David didn't ignore God's call to confession. "Then David said to Nathan, 'I have sinned against the LORD'" (2 Samuel 12:13).

Though David's sin resulted in some difficult consequences and discipline from the Lord, his repentance brought about a renewed relationship with God: "After he had washed, put on lotions and changed his clothes, he went into the house of the LORD and worshiped" (2 Samuel 12:20).

Perhaps it was at that time that David wrote these words about confession and the joy of being honest before God:

> Then I acknowledged my sin to you and did not cover up my iniquity. I said, "I will confess my transgressions to the LORD"—and you forgave the guilt of my sin.... Rejoice in the LORD and be glad, you righteous; sing all you who are upright in heart! (Psalm 32:5, 11)

Even though David suffered for his sin, the freedom of stepping out of his cell and being "upright in heart" brought rejoicing. God turned David's mourning into gladness.

Confession is a crucial part of God's covenant with us. At salvation, confession is an expression of our understanding that we need a Savior. If we refuse to accept that we are sinners, we cannot be born again. After the new birth, confession indicates our willingness to be molded into our Savior's image. If we insist on hiding sin from God, we cannot grow up spiritually.

I believe that honesty and humility are closely related. Being honest and open to others about our failures and hurts engenders a humble spirit. And humility is a guarantee of God's grace: "God opposes the proud but gives grace to the humble" (James 4:6).

After many years of living with the lie I had told when I was sixteen, I wanted to be set free from my prison. I wanted a clear conscience, and I wanted to grow up—to be molded into the image of Jesus Christ. That's what drove me to finally tell the truth to my family and friends.

In God's time, and after much prayer, He gave me the courage to reveal my secret sin. One by one, my fears fell away until I had made full confession. The enemy lost the battle. Was there fallout? Some. Did telling my secret live up to my fears? Not even close. In fact, there have been more blessings than I can count. As Proverbs 28:13 says, "He who conceals his sins does not prosper, but whoever confesses and renounces them finds mercy."

Unveiling the part of my heart that I had vowed I would always conceal turned out to be one of the most important things I have ever done. Why? I can sum up the answer in one word—*freedom*. That lie was the lock on my prison cell. When I confessed my sin, not only was I set free from my self-imposed sentence, but God also began to unlock, and then open, my heart and mind. Scriptures that before had seemed obscure suddenly made sense. Love and grace that had been hard for me to give now flowed freely. My relationship with God and the bonds with my family grew stronger than ever because they were based on truth. As my relationships became more genuine, I began to feel more authentic. I no longer felt broken; I felt whole. My hurt was finally healing, and gladness was taking the place of mourning. In God's mysterious way, He was turning my regret into joy. When that happened, it ceased to be regret.

WISE DISCLOSURE

Should *every* secret be revealed? To God, yes! Of course, we aren't telling the Lord anything He doesn't already know. St. Augustine said:

O Lord, the depths of man's conscience lie bare before your eyes. Could anything of mine remain hidden from you, even if I refused to confess it? I should only be shielding my eyes from seeing you, not hiding myself from you.[2]

Confession doesn't change God; it changes us. We don't enlighten *Him* about our sin and regret. When we confess, God enlightens *us* with deeper understanding of His mercy. But that enlightenment comes only when darkness is exposed.

If we claim to have fellowship with him yet walk in the darkness, we lie and do not live by the truth. But if we walk in the light, as he is in the light, we have fellowship with one another, and the blood of Jesus, his Son, purifies us from all sin. (1 John 1:6–7)

Our fellowship with God is based solely on His grace. We cannot grow in grace that remains concealed, and God cannot reveal His grace unless we bare ourselves before Him. Tell God everything. Period. No exceptions.

On the other hand, we must be cautious and wise about revealing secret sin, private pain, or hidden regret to *other people*. Often what is in question is not *whether* to confess, but *to whom* to confess. We must be careful about whom we trust and what we say. Careless or unwise disclosure of shocking information has shattered countless families and can be particularly harmful for children. We need a large measure of both gentleness and prudence. There is a huge difference between *unfolding* the truth and *unleashing* it.

Depending on the situation, you will find differing opinions about what to confess to whom. For example, in answer to the question of whether an unfaithful partner who has repented should reveal a secret affair to his or her spouse, authors Tim and Beverly LaHaye recommend having only "an honest talk with one's minister."[3] However, Christian counselor H. Norman Wright says, "You should tell your [spouse] if you have an affair."[4] John MacArthur has this to say:

> Confession of guilt must *always* be made to God. Confession is also owed to whomever our sin has injured. The arena of confession should be as large as the audience of the original offense. Public transgressions call for public confession; private sins should be confessed to God alone.[5]

So how do you know if you need to confess your wrongdoing to someone other than God? Although every person and situation is unique, here are five general guidelines:

1. *You feel that what you are hiding is hindering your relationships with others.* Do your relationships seem to reach a certain level and then stop growing? Does true intimacy seem out of your reach? Do you avoid fellowship with other believers because you don't want them to see you too clearly? Isolation leads to desolation.
2. *You are hiding a sin that you have been unable to conquer on your own.* Do you tell God that you'll do anything to overcome your sin and then remain in the darkness because you're embarrassed? Maybe God is not withholding power from you; maybe He intends to give you strength through another member of His body.

3. *You aren't living with unconfessed sin, but the consequence of a past sin or situation remains a secret and could be revealed haphazardly, causing great harm to innocent parties.* It may be better to tell the truth proactively, but gently, so that you or someone else won't blurt it out indiscriminately.

4. *Your silence prevents full repentance.* Repenting in your heart merely precedes repentant behavior; it doesn't replace it. Although my heart was repentant for the lie I told at sixteen, I wasn't fully repentant until I no longer perpetuated the lie. Sometimes confession to others is our only means of untangling the web.

5. *You feel constant remorse or some other emotional pain over your secret, and it keeps you mired in the muck of regret.* When we confess our secret sins and hidden regrets, we open the door for grace to enter our lives.

If none of these descriptions applies to you, untold secrets may not be a source of pain for you. But if any of them does fit your situation, chances are that there is at least one source of regret in your life. Prayerfully consider whom God has prepared to hear the pain in your heart.

If the thought of confession to another person petrifies you, be at peace. Confession doesn't have to mean public shame and humiliation. The purposes for confession are to repent fully and receive grace, help, and healing—not to be the star of a public lynching. Even if your secret is such that it will eventually require the public to become aware of it, you should first confess it privately to at least one mature Christian. This person should be capable of giving you grace, godly advice, moral support, and confidentiality.

A wise biblical counselor once told me, "We should always be careful to whom we make ourselves vulnerable."[6] Notice he did not say, "Don't be vulnerable," but rather "be careful." If you feel the need to reveal a secret to another person, some good choices might be:

- clergy
- counselors
- mentors
- parents
- siblings
- support groups
- a trusted friend (proven over time)

Whomever you choose, this person should be a mature believer. It is usually best not to entrust sensitive or personal information to nonbelievers or immature Christians. First, they probably aren't equipped to help you, so it's not fair to put them in that position. Second, you may cause them to stumble by setting a poor example.

Other people you should *not* consider as confidants:

- new friends
- children (You may have to reveal something to them, but they should not be your advisors.)
- subordinates at work or in ministry (You set the example for your subordinates, and you seek accountability from your authority.)

Almost as important as *whom* you choose to tell is *when* you choose to tell. As soon as you have made the decision to be open and have chosen a confidant, make a point of confessing as soon as possible. Set up an appointment if that will help you follow through. If you make the decision and then don't do it when you are calm, you may end up blurting out the truth in an emotional moment—perhaps to the wrong person.

Don't overestimate how much time you have. If you have a secret sin that you need help overcoming and feel like you're riding an out-of-control snowball, confess before you crash. Doing so will give you the help you need to steer clear of obstacles. It is much less painful for everyone concerned if you confess before your secret is discovered. Besides that, confession gives you greater control of how your story is revealed. I'd much rather enter my plea and submit my case with a lawyer at my side than be publicly arrested and tried in the media before I'm ever heard. Take control while you can. You may not be able to forever.

So is there ever a time when you *shouldn't* confess? Yes: when your confession is really meant as a challenge to others to accept your behavior. Some people so justify their actions that they begin to see the *secret*—not the sin—as the problem. These people don't have broken and contrite hearts in search of grace and help. They reveal their secret for selfish reasons—to free themselves to sin openly and even to dare others to love them unconditionally. They say, "Here I am; deal with it." They don't want acceptance *in spite of* their sin; they want acceptance *because of* it. This is not true confession.

Keep in mind the four *c*'s of repentance: *conviction, confession, contrition,* and *conversion.* If repentance isn't your desire, then save your confession until it is. In the meantime, don't forget that fifth *c*— the *consequences* that come from sin.

Even if you confess from a truly contrite heart, you must be prepared for the consequence of your sin. Unfortunately, other people don't always understand—or forgive. Sometimes the whole truth means broken relationships. Often restitution is costly. What if you struggle with a secret because you know that confession will mean that all of your worst fears *will* come true? Your decision will depend on the degree of freedom you desire. Overcoming regret that's caused by hidden sin or pain will require authenticity. *Someone* needs to know the real you. Do you really want to be free from regret? Do you want out of your prison?

A confessed and convicted criminal on death row can feel freer than a Wall Street executive harboring a secret. Chains may bind the one, but in his heart he has wings. The other flies everywhere in his private jet, but in his heart he is shackled to a secret. Freedom can be found in physical prisons. It's the spiritual ones we should fear the most.

When we choose to stay in our cell, we choose isolation, darkness, and spiritual paralysis. Authentic living, however, while it may involve consequences for our sin, restores us to fellowship, light, and spiritual victory. It allows God to work in us to lovingly mold us in the image of His Son. Which would you rather experience?

Giving Up

Do you harbor untold grief? Pain you think you must keep private and bear alone? Sins you'd rather keep secret? Your sins may not be adultery and murder, to which David confessed, or even the one I told Debra about—pride. They could be the lewd movies you watch in secret, the deceitful deals you make at work, or the profanity you use everywhere except in the pew. Or maybe it's a sin you dealt with long ago, but its concealed consequences keep you imprisoned in sorrow and silence.

If so, know that the Lord will point out the dark places in your life. He *will* convict you. When He does, you will face a decision: Remain in darkness or step into the light. Like me, you may wrestle with God. But it's much less painful to give up quickly. Ask Him to help you be willing to make confession, for "if we confess our sins, he is faithful and just and will forgive us our sins and purify us from all unrighteousness" (1 John 1:9). As we choose to be accountable to one another, we will find healing in the humbling words, "Confess your sins to each other and pray for each other so that you may be healed" (James 5:16).

One way or another, God will bring discipline. Why? Because He bought *all* of us with the blood of His Son, and He wants to heal all of us spiritually. He wants to teach us, use us, and make us holy. He wants the world to see "plainly that what [you have] done has been done through God" (John 3:21). Confession brings restoration, and restored human beings bring glory and honor to God.

Is freedom calling you? Remember that you are the one who locked the door of your cell and that you still hold the key. Pray for release. Then ask the Great Physician to arrange a divine appointment for you with someone to whom you can tell the truth and set yourself free.

7

No Ax to Grind

Anger and Forgiveness

🌿 I'VE KNOWN Laura and her brother Gary since we were kids, and over the years I've tried to support them as they've dealt with the repercussions of an incredibly abusive childhood.

Their mother was an alcoholic, a drug abuser, and a pathological liar who neglected and abused them regularly. She turned a blind eye and refused to intervene when the man who was her husband at the time molested Laura. She deceived Gary, and he unwittingly helped her break into their neighbor's house. The police arrested him along with her. Later, she sent him to a prisonlike "reform" school where he was beaten and abused. Understandably, Laura and Gary carried lots of anger into adulthood.

Now in their twenties, Laura and Gary have been estranged

from their mother for many years. Recently, they learned that she was dying. On the day they heard this news, they each called me—without the other's knowledge—to talk about their mother.

Both Laura and Gary told me that they've made choices in their lives they deeply regret and that when they analyze those choices, they realize that most of them can be traced in some way to their mother. Her bad choices had influenced most of their own.

Laura was not saddened by the news of her mother's illness, but she did find terrible pain and anger churning within her as old memories flooded her mind. Gary had a different reaction—he was completely indifferent to the news. Yet his indifference disturbed him because he realized it was rooted in bitterness.

Their words revealed their need to get past their past.

Laura said, "Something inside tells me that if I'm going to survive and move on, I have to find a way to let go of all this anger and resentment." And Gary told me, "What that woman did to me still affects how I make decisions. There's no way I'm going to let her have another swipe at me just because she's dying." Laura's still in pain. Gary's still a victim. Both still suffer from regret. And there is only one remedy: forgiveness.

SOUL-POLLUTION

If you're trying to get past *your* past, why does forgiving the sins of other people matter? Because if we don't forgive other people for how they have negatively influenced our choices, we will never overcome our resentment and therefore never be able to move beyond old wounds and hurts.

As important as that is, it's not the main reason we should forgive others. We are to forgive primarily because God commands us to do so. Many Scriptures echo Colossians 3:13: "Bear with each other and forgive whatever grievances you may have against one another. Forgive as the Lord forgave you." When we don't obey that command, we suffer a multitude of lingering consequences—including an inability to overcome regret. In *The Freedom and Power of Forgiveness,* Dr. John MacArthur writes:

> Unforgivingness is a toxin. It poisons the heart and mind with bitterness, distorting one's whole perspective on life. Anger, resentment, and sorrow begin to overshadow and overwhelm the unforgiving person—a kind of soul-pollution that enflames evil appetites and evil emotions.[1]

Those evil appetites and emotions not only keep us from conquering regret *in the present,* they also lead us to decisions that will cause more regret *in the future.*

I believe that a refusal to forgive leaves at least four kinds of residue:

- *Bitterness.* Have you ever known a bitter person who is truly happy? Bitter people may *look and act* happy, but beneath the surface they are angry and in deep pain. Bitterness is ugly. It can make a woman hard and turn a man into a tyrant.
- *Blame.* It's easy for Gary and Laura to blame their mother for some of the poor decisions they've made. No one can deny that these two entered adulthood with profound emotional scars that hindered their ability to make good

choices. Yet when you blame someone else for what *you* have chosen to do, your past mistakes become tangled up with someone else's. It's hard to get past your past when it's not just your past you're dealing with.

- *Pain.* It is impossible to let go of the pain that others have caused if you still want to punish them for inflicting it. And if you refuse to forgive until the offender understands and apologizes for the pain he or she has caused, you may be waiting forever. Some pain can be released *only* through forgiveness.

- *Victim mentality.* If you hurt me, I'm not just *the* victim— I'm *your* victim. But if I forgive you, you no longer have that power over me. I'm no longer connected to you because I take ownership and control of my life—hurts, bad circumstances, and all.

These by-products of withholding forgiveness only keep us focused on the past and, therefore, tethered to regret. Forgiveness, however, can dispel the negative feelings that lead to soul-pollution. When we forgive, we separate ourselves from offenses, and the farther offenses are from us, the easier it is to forget them. In fact, our *willingness to forgive* will directly impact our *ability to forget*. We may never be able to totally forget what has happened in the past—to us or because of us—but forgiveness allows us to stop reliving it. Pain then begins to subside, and the offense drifts from the forefront of our minds. Through forgiveness, the past loses its power over us, and usually we are able to forget things we thought we never could.

FORGIVENESS: WHAT IT'S NOT
AND WHAT KEEPS US FROM IT

Forgiveness is not what many people think it is. It isn't denying an offense. It isn't a brief acknowledgment, followed by a well-rehearsed Christian platitude like "It's okay. I've left it at the foot of the cross." It isn't shrugging off a hurtful experience—"Oh, well. You probably didn't realize what you were doing."

Neither is forgiveness a feeling, although it has many feelings associated with it. In and of itself, it is not an emotion, nor does it depend on our emotions. Sometimes we think, *If I forgive, then I won't hurt.* Eventually, that might be true. But rarely do painful feelings leave the moment you choose to forgive someone.

Finally, forgiveness does not necessarily bring reconciliation, though that is one of its main goals. Therefore, it does not depend on the other people acknowledging their wrongdoing or being sorry for it.

Often it is a desire to receive something from our offenders that keeps us from forgiving. We feel that they owe us—an admission, explanation, apology, understanding—and until they pay us in full, we refuse to forgive them. When we don't get what we seek, we pile more anger on top of what we already feel because of the offense.

Laura and Gary have harbored resentment and withheld forgiveness because they feel a need to *receive* something from their mother. Laura wants so badly for her mother to understand how hurtful her actions have been and to be sorry for them. She has screamed the truth at her mother many times, but her screams have fallen on deaf ears. Apart from a miracle, Laura's mother will never understand. The result is that there is a huge barrier, not only between Laura and her mother, but also between Laura and her own healing. The same goes for Gary. He wants his mother to own up to her mistakes, and since she won't, he feels no compulsion to forgive. He holds on to his ill will—and remains mired in regret.

I believe that there is one solution to both anger and the desire to receive something from those who offend us. It's not found in rehashing or endlessly analyzing what they did and how we responded; it's found in the story about the woman caught in adultery. The scribes and Pharisees condemned the woman, but Jesus changed their attitude by shifting their focus from her to themselves. We can find a greater capacity to extend grace if we, too, take our eyes off the offender and examine ourselves. When we do that, our perspective of our offender can change..

Let's take a closer look at how we should respond when we desire to receive something from our offender or when we find ourselves with unresolved anger.

A Desire to Receive

Instead of focusing on the understanding or the apology that they want from their mother, Laura and Gary need to look at themselves. It's difficult to examine our failures honestly, because our instinct is to look at everyone *except* ourselves. Adam and Eve certainly did that in the Garden of Eden. When God confronted them with their sin, He looked at Adam, Adam looked at Eve, and Eve looked at the serpent (see Genesis 3). When Laura and Gary look at themselves, they will begin to understand that they, just like their mother, have hurt others and haven't known how much. We all have.

We find an even more powerful reason for Laura and Gary—

and all of us—to give up the desire to receive from our offender when we look at our relationship to Christ. Jesus did not wait for us to apologize or understand the pain we had caused Him before He offered to forgive us. Even after we accept His forgiveness, do we ever really understand how much we hurt Him? Do we understand how He felt to be misunderstood, despised, rejected, and tortured to death? Do we understand the agony He bore knowing that He didn't deserve any of it? Of course we don't. Did our lack of understanding stop Him from forgiving us? No way. If He had waited for us to understand before He forgave, we would all be doomed.

If you are waiting to forgive those who have offended you until you receive something from them, keep in mind two things. First, by doing this, you ultimately give them control over your behavior. And second, because they may never give you what you want, you give them that power over you forever.

Anger

Laura and Gary are angry that their mother doesn't understand, and they are angry about years of abuse and neglect. Their anger is certainly justified, but if they hold on to it, they will (and have) become increasingly miserable. Finding a way to let go of their anger is not for their mother's sake, but for their own. Anger is painful. Letting go of it is painful. But in the end, releasing anger brings relief.

If we continually replay or analyze the hurt that has been inflicted on us, we will never find the motivation or strength to let go of anger. Freedom from anger begins when we look closely at ourselves and at the forgiveness we have received from Christ. When I was dealing with anger that I couldn't get rid of, more than

one person told me, "Just leave your anger at the foot of the cross."
How I hated that phrase! I often wondered if the people who said
it even knew what it meant—I sure didn't. Whether they were
spouting platitudes or pointing me back to the truth, the fact
remains: On the cross Jesus had given me grace; therefore, I needed
to extend it to those who had hurt me. I didn't deserve God's grace
and neither did my offenders, but grace is what God was calling me
to give because grace is what I had been given. When you truly
understand your own sinfulness and the undeserved generosity
that God has granted you, anger at other people either instantly dis-
appears or slowly begins to wane.

When that happens, you realize that it is possible to hate what
someone has done without hating the person. As C. S. Lewis put it:

> For a long time I used to think this a silly, straw-splitting
> distinction: how could you hate what a man did and not
> hate the man? But years later it occurred to me that there
> was one man to whom I had been doing this all my life—
> namely myself. However much I might dislike my own
> cowardice or conceit or greed, I went on loving myself.
> There had never been the slightest difficulty about it. In
> fact, the very reason why I hated the things was that I loved
> the man. Just because I loved myself, I was sorry to find
> that I was the sort of man who did those things.[2]

In some ways, it is because Laura and Gary loved their mother
that she could hurt them so deeply. If they will realize that and also
begin to understand the depth of the forgiveness they have received
from Christ, they will feel the anger at their mother begin to ebb. Their

anger at her *sin* may remain, but it will be the same anger they feel for all sin. Most importantly, a roadblock to forgiveness will be removed.

LET 'EM OFF THE HOOK?

Sometimes we are afraid to forgive because we think that letting offenders off our hook means letting them off God's hook too. Nothing could be farther from the truth. A transgression against us is above all a transgression against God. When we let go of offenses, we put the business where it should be—squarely between the offender and God—and we take ourselves out of the middle.

Our sense of justice often keeps us in the middle because the thought of forgiveness violates it. How can it be right to just let someone walk away unpunished? The problem is that our notion of justice is flawed—and that's precisely the reason we should let our offender go. God is far better at meting out justice than we are. In *What's So Amazing About Grace?* Philip Yancey says:

> In the final analysis, forgiveness is an act of faith. By forgiving another, I am trusting that God is a better justice-maker than I am. By forgiving, I release my own right to get even and leave all issues of fairness for God to work out. I leave in God's hands the scales that must balance justice and mercy…. Though wrong does not disappear when I forgive, it loses its grip on me and is taken over by God, who knows what to do.[3]

In essence, we give grace the same way we receive it—*by faith*. There's another important reason why we have to get out from between God and our offender: Refusing to forgive another person actually puts *us* in the hot seat with God. Lack of forgiveness is itself a sin, and when we sin, we are subject to God's chastisement. As Hebrews 12:6 says, "The Lord disciplines those he loves, and he punishes everyone he accepts as a son." If our perfect Father can forgive the offense and offender who has hurt us, who are we to withhold our forgiveness? John MacArthur says:

> Christians who fail to show mercy will be subject to divine chastisement without much mercy. I am convinced that multitudes of Christians who suffer from stress, depression, discouragement, relationship problems, and all sorts of other hardships experience those things because of a refusal to forgive.[4]

Why is refusing to forgive a sin? Because forgiving other people is based on what we ourselves have received. We have been shown mercy; therefore, God requires that we show it to others. I've heard some people justify their lack of mercy by saying, "Well, God never had to forgive *me* for anything *this* bad, so He doesn't expect me to forgive." That statement is a form of stone throwing based on ignorance of one's own sinfulness, and it misses the point of God's command to forgive. In God's eyes we are all sinners, and we will never have to forgive another as much as God has forgiven us—no matter what someone else has done.

That's what the scribes and Pharisees realized when they couldn't cast the first stone at the woman caught in adultery. They may or may not have been adulterers, but they knew they were sinners—period.

Because refusing to forgive is a sin, forgiveness is often a form of repentance. So when you forgive, it could be that the person you let off the hook is yourself.

IT'S MY PARTY

In chapter 3, I told how when I was in my teens, self-confidence masked my pride. Sometimes withholding forgiveness disguises itself as two other forms of pride—self-pity and self-righteousness. See a pattern? A focus on *self* causes all of these problems.

John MacArthur says:

> Pride, I am convinced, is the primary reason most people refuse to forgive. They nurse self-pity (which is nothing but a form of pride). Their ego is wounded, and they will not stand for that. Prideful reactions to an offense can run the gamut from those who simply wallow in self-pity to those who retaliate with an even worse offense. All such responses are wrong because they are motivated by pride.[5]

Self-pity

When my husband was dying, there was nothing I disliked more than to have people pity me. I didn't feel sorry for myself, and I didn't want others to, either. The reason I hated it so much was because it stood in stark contrast to what I knew to be true: God didn't feel sorry for me. If God was in control of my family, then I certainly wasn't a victim. Pity made me look like a victim.

Self-pity does the same thing. It leads us to look at ourselves as victims and reveals that we don't really believe that God is sovereign. God is Lord over everything—including those who hurt us.

He allows offenses and hurts to come into our life for His purpose. We don't have to know that purpose; we have to trust the Person who allowed it. That was Christ's attitude when He went to the cross. He was willing to endure incredible suffering for our sin because He trusted His Father completely.

Another problem with self-pity is that although it might seem to be caused by dwelling *too much* on our losses, it actually keeps us from accepting them. In essence, self-pity is loss mixed with pride and resentment, which prevent us from completely accepting our loss because blame, anger, or a sense of victimization diverts our attention. Accepting loss on an emotional level is an important part of conquering regret—so important that a couple of chapters of this book are dedicated to the subject. We must accept *all* of the losses of our past in order to move forward.

When we don't forgive, our grief is selfish—a pity party—and incomplete. For example, if a husband refuses to forgive his wife for adultery and then divorces her, he may grieve the loss of the relationship ("She failed me, so I'm losing part of the dream for my life"), but he will not fully realize the loss of the *person*. He'll remain stuck because he never acknowledges all of his losses. Forgiving her allows him to grieve for all that he has lost. "She failed me, so I'm losing my dream *and* I'm losing *her*."

Ironically, in a case like this, only when the husband lays aside self-pity and forgives will he be able to see that if he had forgiven sooner, the marriage could have been saved despite the adultery. Only when he stops blaming his wife will he be able to see that he failed as well—even if only in not forgiving her sooner. She was unfaithful. He was unforgiving. Why did the marriage really end?

Many marriages end because of unrepentant unfaithfulness. I

believe that even more end because of unrepentant unforgiving-ness. And often the unforgiving spouse doesn't even see it, because self-pity and blame are in the way.

I love Chuck Swindoll's rationale for laying aside self-pity and blame:

> It was because David refused to take vengeance on King Saul that we remember his story…. It was because Joseph was so willing to forgive his brothers that we admire him…. And it was because Job did not waver in his faith…that we are impressed to this day.
>
> If you'd just as soon be forgotten because you lived consumed with blame and self-pity, keep fighting back. Get even. Stay angry. But if you hope to be remembered, admired, and rewarded, press on even though you've been ripped off.[6]

When I looked through the eyes of bitterness at how others' mistakes related to my own, I condemned them and pitied myself. Only when I began to look through the eyes of love did I learn to show grace to the other person and take responsibility for myself.

Self-righteousness

Why is it that so often when someone sins against us, we oppose their wrong with a list of our rights? We have the right to be mad. We have the right to punish them. We have the right to condemn them because *we've* never done *that*. Philip Yancey said, "The opposite of sin is grace, not virtue."[7] It was grace, not our virtue, that brought us forgiveness.

Self-righteous condemnation was the problem when the

scribes and Pharisees brought the woman caught in adultery to Jesus to be judged. It was only after Jesus forced them to admit to themselves that they were sinners just like her that they stopped condemning her. They pointed their finger—Jesus held up a mirror.

As believers, we know that if it weren't for Christ, nothing about us would be righteous. Yet when it comes time to forgive, we forget. We act like we have nothing to give, when in fact the opposite is true. Our Father has been so generous with us that we are rich in the ability to show mercy. Too often we don't treat each other with the "kindness meant to lead to repentance," as our Father deals with us, but with disdain, judgment, and self-righteous indignation.

In the introduction to *Jane Eyre,* Charlotte Bronte says this: "Conventionality is not morality. Self-righteousness is not religion. To attack the first is not to assail the last. To pluck the mask from the face of the Pharisee is not to lift an impious hand to the Crown of Thorns."[8] In other words, judging that others are wrong is not the same as being right. Being right means coming full circle and extending grace.

That truth is vitally important when someone you care about has a confession to make.

THE SECRET CONNECTION

Philip Yancey wrote *What's So Amazing About Grace?* because of a story he had heard from a friend who was a reporter. A homeless, drug-addicted prostitute with a hungry and abused child had gone to the reporter looking for help. When he asked her if she'd ever gone to church for help, she replied, "Church! Why would I ever go there? I was already feeling terrible about myself. They'd just make me feel worse."[9]

I am convinced that the reason most people keep painful secrets is not because they want to deceive, but because they have a feeling akin to that of the desperate, drug-abusing mother in Yancey's book—a feeling that they have nobody to whom they can turn for acceptance. They believe that they can't find anyone who won't reject, punish, or judge them.

In some circles, it is *Christians* who have the worst reputation for being judgmental, unforgiving, and ungracious. What makes that incredibly odd is that the very people we reject are the kind Jesus hung out with—those known for their failure. Somewhere in our transition from paupers to princes we've become more like the Pharisees that Jesus avoided. We have conformed to the standards of the Christian community and called ourselves righteous, forgetting that it was our need that put us in that community in the first place.

Unbelievers with secrets often don't believe that the body of Christ is the place to look for mercy, and neither do many Christians. Are you so aware of the grace you've received that others feel safe to confess their most painful sins to you? Do others know you as one who doesn't condemn, but as one who offers grace and help? When grace sets you free, you will set others free.

THE MARKS OF FORGIVENESS

Forgiveness is a choice. We make it for several reasons: It is a command from God; it mirrors the mercy we have been given; it is the only way to be released from the pain another has caused us; and it is the only way to totally overcome regret. I like the definition of forgiveness offered by Neil T. Anderson:

> Forgiveness is agreeing to live with the consequences of another person's sin. Forgiveness is costly; we pay the price of the evil we forgive. Yet you're going to live with those consequences whether you want to or not; your only choice is whether you will do so in the bitterness of withholding forgiveness or the freedom of offering forgiveness. That's how Jesus forgave you—He took the consequences of your sin upon Himself. All true forgiveness is substitutional, because no one really forgives without bearing the penalty of the other person's sin.[10]

Laura and Gary *will* live with the consequences of their mother's sin. Whether or not they stay fettered to it because of their unwillingness to forgive is up to them. The same is true for you and me. We will live with the consequences of other people's sin, just as they will live with the consequences of ours. Staying bound to the pain of an offense, however, is optional.

Forgiveness is the repentance that puts us right with God, releases our pain, and spins us around on the road of life so that we face forward. Its benefits are undeniable. One of the most important things about it is that it's part of fulfilling our calling to follow Christ. That's not an easy calling, but neither was Christ's. His desire to forgive us essentially required Him to drive nails into His own hands. If we are to be Christlike, then our marks will be like His—

the scars of sacrifice, not the scars of resentment. Forgiveness is also painful. It costs us a great deal, and the price is high because it has great value. Forgiveness is never cheap or easy, but whether you are the giver or the receiver, the freedom it brings is always worth it.

RESOLVING THE IRRESOLVABLE

My friend Kim has a problem. As a child, she was abandoned by her mother and abused by her father and grandmother. When she was growing up, she made many choices she later regretted. She has forgiven her father and grandmother for influencing her poor decisions, but they refuse to forgive her for some hurtful things she did. Kim's problem isn't *giving* forgiveness, but *getting* it. Her family bombards her with phrases like "I'll never forgive *you*"; "You *used* to be my favorite"; and "We can *never* be the same again." They also tell her, "Your life could have been so much better." Kim continues to feel guilty because she can't get the forgiveness that she craves from her family, and it keeps her stuck in her past. She has repeatedly asked for, and been denied, forgiveness.

How do we deal with the condemnation of loved ones? Romans 12:18 says, "If it is possible, as far as it depends on you, live at peace with everyone." Kim has asked her family for forgiveness and done everything she knows how to do to make amends. Though reconciliation is *always* the goal of forgiveness, if forgiveness is one-sided, reconciliation isn't always possible.

If we have done all we can to live at peace with everyone, then we needn't feel guilty over someone else's lack of forgiveness. We may have to grieve the loss of relationships, which is what Kim has to do. Though Kim hates losing the relationship with her father and grandmother, it has become impossible to live in peace because they continue to sin by not forgiving.

STILL MAD AT THE PERSON IN THE MIRROR?

"I know that God forgives me, but I can't forgive myself." I've heard that phrase from many people who believe that self-forgiveness is needed to overcome their past. But self-forgiveness is not mentioned one time in the Bible. There's a reason for that.

God doesn't just forgive—He pronounces us *not guilty*. If we are no longer guilty, for what do we need to forgive ourselves? If we understand and receive *God's* forgiveness, forgiving ourselves isn't necessary, and neither are self-punishment and unending despair. If we persist in punishing ourselves, we are refusing God's forgiveness. In essence, we are saying that His provision of a Savior wasn't enough. We buy into the subtle lie that we can become righteous through self-suffering, when in truth we can become righteous only through Christ's suffering.

Sometimes we stay mad at ourselves not because we haven't forgiven someone, but because our forgiveness was late in coming. Not having forgiven *sooner* is the source of our regret. The consequences of being slow to forgive can be devastating. There are relationships that could have known more joy if they had known more grace. There are affairs, which if they had been forgiven, needn't have led to divorce. There are parents who could have forgiven or known forgiveness before they died.

If forgiving too late is the source of your regret, your problem is no longer unforgivingness. It is guilt. Remorse over failure to forgive is no different than any other kind of regret because sin is sin. It doesn't matter whether what you regret is adultery, lies, an abortion—or withholding forgiveness. God's grace covers them all. If you have repented from your unwillingness to forgive, you are not only forgiven, you are not guilty.

Of course, as with any sin, the failure to forgive can have painful consequences. Many times, God disciplines and trains us by using the painful consequences of our sin. Hebrews 12:11–12 says, "No discipline seems pleasant at the time, but painful. Later on, however, it produces a harvest of righteousness and peace for those who have been trained by it. Therefore, strengthen your feeble arms and weak knees." But even knowing that we are being trained doesn't relieve the pain of consequences we can't change. For me, such pain often felt pointless, and the permanent consequences of my failures tormented me because I felt like I had messed up God's plan for my life.

In the next couple of chapters, we will take a look at how you can have a renewed sense of purpose even as you endure the consequences of sin. We'll also look at how long-term consequences fit into God's plans and what you can do if you think you've messed up His plan for you.

8

Diving for Pearls

Searching the Mysteries of the Deep

❧ AS I have tried to figure out God's plan for my life, I have spent considerable time asking "why?" Why was I born into a certain family at a particular time in history? Why didn't I receive the love, training, and opportunities during childhood that some of my friends did? Why wasn't I better equipped to make good choices? I have wanted to understand God's placement *of* me so I could figure out His use *for* me.

I have wondered how much influence God has had over my circumstances. Did He order the steps of my life? Or have nothing to do with them? If He did have something to do with directing me, did He do this my whole life or only after I was saved? How much of my circumstances are due to Satan, our fallen world, or my own flesh?

More than anything, I have wanted to know God's plan for *me*. Why did God create *me* in the first place? How do *I* fit into His greater plan? What is *my* purpose within God's purpose? And most importantly, have my sinful choices changed God's plan for me?

Questions about the meaning of existence are an intrinsic part of life. We long for metaphysical answers here on terra firma. Pain, including regret, seems to intensify and complicate our questions. We not only want to know "why," but also "why me?"

In my attempt to find answers to such questions, I have discovered two profound truths that have helped me get past my past: The first is that life, in terms of God's grand plan, is not about me or my questions. The second is that questions are a great place to begin to experience the essence of life—knowing God.

I'M NOT THE POINT

Because I was so filled with regret about my past, I began to grill God with earnest questions. I queried Him in prayer and searched His Word for answers. I wanted Him to explain how not only my failures and their consequences, but also the circumstances of life over which I had no control fit into the big scheme of things.

Much to my frustration, it seemed that God didn't feel obliged to tell me. The harder I looked for answers, the more elusive they became, and I ended up with only more questions. It seemed that they would forever stand between God and me. I cried out in my journal:

There simply are no answers for some of life's questions. Is my quest for answers doomed to be an exercise in futility? Is heaven silent? Must we live forever with problems that have no solutions? Are we doomed to live with pain we cannot resolve because we do not know its source? I feel like a child in a dark room and the light switch is too high on the wall. I keep jumping up trying to turn on the light, hoping maybe today is the day I have grown enough to reach.

Even as I despaired of finding answers, I continued to look for them. Gradually, however, I came to realize that the lack of answers to my questions wasn't what stood between God and me. Jesus said, "Love the Lord your God with all your heart and with all your soul and with all your mind and with all your strength." And, "'Love your neighbor as yourself.' There is no commandment greater than these" (Mark 12:30–31). His words showed me that my real problem was *me*. My focus hadn't been on either God or my neighbor. I was focused almost completely on myself. My priority was wrong. Not only am I not first, I'm a distant third behind God and everybody else. Oh, my intellect had acknowledged that life was bigger than my desires and struggles, but my questions betrayed my heart.

According to Jesus, my passion needed to be for God and other people. Regret, however, focused my passion on my past, my pain, and myself. It perpetuated my not-so-subtle, prideful, self-centered notion that life is all about me.

HE IS THE POINT

Questions are a springboard to getting to know God. I often think that I am focused on God, but when I look a little more closely, I see that I am actually focused on my desire to have Him come in and fix my painful life, or at least answer for it. I have to struggle to remember that God isn't there to ease my suffering when I call; rather, my suffering is there to draw me closer to Him. Questions about life and purpose are a part of that. Paradoxically, to receive answers to our questions, we have to stop focusing on finding the answers, because they don't pull us from the quicksand of regret. Knowing God does.

As we seek Him, the answers may come—or they may not. God responded to me not by directly answering my questions, but by revealing Himself and asking me to trust Him. God doesn't want our pain to make us more concerned with ourselves, but to make us aware of our desperate need of Him. In *Knowing God,* J. I. Packer says:

> What were we made for? To know God. What aim should we set ourselves in life? To know God. What is the "eternal life" that Jesus gives? Knowledge of God. "This is life eternal, that they might know thee the only true God, and Jesus Christ, whom thou has sent" (John 17:3, KJV). What is the best thing in life, bringing more joy, delight, and contentment, than anything else? Knowledge of God.[1]

In order to have any lasting contentment or joy, we *need* to know God—not as we have *thought* Him to be or as we *want* Him to be, but as He has *revealed* Himself in His Word and through His works. A. W. Tozer said:

That our idea of God correspond as nearly as possible to the true being of God is of immense importance to us. Compared with our actual thoughts about him, our creedal statements are of little consequence. Our real idea of God may lie buried under the rubbish of conventional religious notions and may require an intelligent and vigorous search before it is finally unearthed and exposed for what it is. Only after an ordeal of painful self-probing are we likely to discover what we actually believe about God.[2]

Our response to regret and the feelings that accompany it will reveal what we really believe about God. My regret forced me to confront my perceptions and misconceptions about God, and it drove me to seek to know Him on a deeper level. Only in knowing God and knowing Him *properly* can we put away regret. More importantly, if we live without ever seeking to know Him, we go through life having missed the whole point.

PEARL DIVING

When I was ten years old, my family visited Marineland, an ocean theme park featuring shows with trained whales, dolphins, and seals. All of that was great, but I recall being more fascinated by an exhibition on pearl diving. Beautiful, petite, Japanese women— who didn't look hearty enough to blow up large balloons—each took a deep breath and then dove to a considerable depth. For long minutes, the audience stood watching spellbound, waiting for the frail-looking women to reappear. Long after the onlookers had exhaled the breaths they'd been holding, the women began to bob to the surface. Their reappearance brought sighs of relief from the crowd and thunderous applause as the divers held up their prize of harvested oysters.

Besides sheer entertainment, the exhibition had two purposes: to display the difficulties of pearl diving and to show the value of pearls. We learned that diving for pearls in the open seas is not an easy thing to do and that the rare beauty of perfect pearls makes them of great value. Pearl diving may be difficult, but to those who want pearls, it's worth the effort. As Robert Browning said, "Are there not two points in the adventure of the diver: One, when a beggar he prepares to plunge; One, when a prince he rises with his pearl."[3]

Searching out the pearls of truth in deep spiritual waters is also hard work. It takes great effort to dive deeply into God's Word to learn how we—and our failures and regrets—fit into His plan. Even so, the rewards are worth it.

The Price

The first thing we must have in order to know God is the motivation to seek Him, and God has provided it for all believers. It's called *life*. Everything around us, good and bad, calls us to seek to know God on a deeper level. We have only to recognize that. Therefore, knowing God is *first* an attitude and *then* an activity.

In 1989, after a major cross-country move and job change, my husband, children, and I spent a few years in what felt like poverty. There were many worse off than we were, but to me it was arduous. We relied on family, friends, and food stamps to get by. We lived in a trailer near some railroad tracks. Other families in our trailer park were in similar circumstances, and we became close friends and cohorts in survival with most of our neighbors. It turned out that a lot of them were Christians. Shirley, Danny, and their children lived next door; Kim, Floyd, and their children lived down the street; and Beth and her children lived across the street. Between us, we had fourteen children.

I had never lived in such need. When a child in the neighborhood was ill, our first response wasn't to make an appointment with the doctor—it was to pray, because prayer was free. Sharing financial resources for doctors or food or light bills was a common occurrence. Our entertainment wasn't the local movie theater. It was sitting on a front porch, talking, drinking iced tea, and watching the cardinals, blue jays, and stray cats play.

We learned many things in poverty. We learned the difference between necessities and luxuries. We learned to wait for things we needed and to be content with what we had. We learned to fear less because we knew we could survive much. But the first and most important thing we learned was that pride was a luxury we couldn't afford. We *needed* God and each other, and we knew it. Needing God and each other wasn't something we decided to do because it was right or good. It was something we did because we wanted to survive.

The attitude of those who seek God is the same attitude that prevailed among my neighbors in the trailer park. It is an attitude of dependence—a realization and acceptance of need. *Demanding answers* is a luxury of the prideful; *wanting God* is a necessity of the humble. We can want a close relationship with God, but we won't be willing to dive very deep for it unless we feel we need to.

The distress of regret can make us acutely aware of our need for God. When we're comfortable, we still need Him, but we don't feel that need as urgently. If there isn't much to motivate us to dive for pearls of truth, knowing God gets shoved to the bottom of our "to do" list—usually right below dusting the rafters in the garage. Of course, it is possible to know our need for God apart from poverty or problems; it's just not as easy. I have been rich and I have been poor, and with regard to being motivated to know God, poor was better.

My friend Linda has a wonderful husband and four beautiful children. She passionately loves the Lord and feels called to several kinds of ministry, including home-schooling her children. Opportunities to serve seem to pile up on her front porch like unretrieved newspapers. It is a constant effort for her to apportion her time wisely. She often feels stretched and strained, and she asks God to show her which activities she should end and which she should continue. Because Linda has learned that she is dependent on God, she doesn't demand that He give her a schedule that will enable her to do everything she feels called to do. She allows her need for wisdom to drive her to God.

Many times she has called me and said, "I am on my face before the Lord, but I still don't know what to do. If God would just tell me which path to follow, I would gladly take it. I only want to please Him." Our conversations frequently end without clear-cut answers. She may still feel frustrated and be searching for specific direction. But our conversations always end in agreement that Linda *is* following the Lord and *is* on the right path. Knowing that, she rests while she waits for answers.

When we cry out to God for help, He meets us where we are. As Philip Yancey says, "Human beings do not readily admit desperation. When they do, the kingdom of heaven draws near."[4]

Once we have the right attitude, we can get about the *activity* of knowing God more intimately. How do we go about this? Consider what J. I. Packer says:

> Knowing God involves, first, listening to God's Word and receiving it as the Holy Spirit interprets it, in application to oneself; second, noting God's nature and character, as His Word and works reveal it; third, accepting His invitations, and doing what He commands; fourth, recognizing, and rejoicing in, the love that He has shown in thus approaching one and drawing one into this divine fellowship.[5]

Jesus was even more specific. He told His disciples, "I am the way and the truth and the life. No one comes to the Father except through me. If you really knew me, you would know my Father as well" (John 14:6–7). Philip didn't understand. He said, "'Lord, show us the Father and that will be enough for us.' Jesus answered: 'Don't you know me, Philip, even after I have been among you such a long time? Anyone who has seen me has seen the Father'" (John 14:8–9).

Knowing God is as simple and as impossible as knowing Jesus. It's simple because the Bible is filled with information about Him and insights into His character; it's impossible because, although the Bible answers many questions about Him, it leaves many more unanswered. So it is with God. There is much that He has revealed, but there's infinitely more that He has left a mystery.

In *The Bondage of the Will*, Martin Luther wrote, "Wherever God hides Himself, and wills to be unknown to us, there we have no concern…God in His own nature and majesty is to be left alone; in this regard, we have nothing to do with Him, nor does He wish us to deal with Him. We have to do with Him as clothed and displayed in His Word...." Clarifying this passage, Luther's translators say, "This means simply that we must listen to and deal with God as He speaks to us in Christ, and not attempt to approach or deal with Him apart from Christ." Luther continues, "We may not debate the secret will of Divine Majesty.... But let man occupy himself with God Incarnate, that is, with Jesus crucified, in whom, as Paul says, are all the treasures of wisdom and knowledge."[6]

Knowing that there are impenetrable mysteries about God is never a valid excuse to ignore Him or refuse to believe in Him. Becoming preoccupied with things that He has deliberately kept hidden comes from pride. To demand that God answer our questions about things He has chosen to keep secret is not only futile; it's aggrogant. What He *has* revealed is sufficient for faith and more that we can ever fully understand. What Luther is saying is that we should use our intellect, curiosity, and creativity to understand and enjoy all that God has given us and then spend our time praising Him for just those things. That alone should keep us busy for...say...eternity.

The Prize

Listing the benefits of knowing God can be as absurd as describing the benefits of a pumping heart. If life is your goal, both are essential and both have beneficial results. One of the results of knowing God is that Christians find fellowship and commonality with each other.

If you've ever left behind Christian friends in one city and joined a community of believers somewhere else, you probably know what I'm talking about. It's possible to move into a new town, find a new church, and have immediate camaraderie with other people because of the things you share in common in the Lord: a changed life and behavior, increased faith and love, a sense of peace and purpose, and a remedy for the profound loneliness of life.

But a kinship with other believers is just one of the prizes of knowing God. There are countless others. In my own relationship with Him, I cherish two things above all. The first is that the more I know God, the more passionate I become about Him, and the more passionate I am about Him, the more I feel my need for Him, and the more truth, love, and mercy I find. I don't live tentatively. I live fearlessly and free.

The second thing I cherish is what I call my "universe alignment moments." These are times when the universe seems to align, and in the blink of an eye, I realize God's truths. I feel like everything becomes clear. Questions don't matter. Regret doesn't matter. Pain doesn't matter. All that matters is truth, love, mercy, and the passion of pursuing God. These are moments when I feel like I can almost grasp the love God has for me, and I am then able to feel love for even my worst enemy.

My journal describes one such moment:

Life is becoming sweet despite some difficult circumstances. I can actually feel Him "growing me up." I am learning how to accept the reality and pain of the physical and emotional world, but not *live* there. He is showing me with greater comprehension how to live Spirit-filled. It is not about understanding the *why* of every human experience. It is about absolute trust and relationship with God.

Nothing in life will make us feel richer or more satisfied than realizing the truths of God. In fact, because of divine fellowship with Him, not only will we never again have to suffer persistent regret, but nothing about us will ever be the same. How could any price be too high for such pearls?

FAUX PEARLS AND FAUX PAS

It is not just important to know God—it is important to know Him as He truly is. When we have ideas about God that aren't true, we have faux pearls, or fakes. And faux pearls lead to faux pas. Misconceptions about God lead us into sin and leave us in regret.

For instance, I might believe that God is loving and compassionate toward me but that He is not involved in the details of my life and is therefore unlikely to help me when I'm in trouble. So if I find myself in a situation that feels hopeless, such as a difficult marriage, my misconception about God's character could easily lead me to believe that He isn't concerned with my pain. I would then most likely be tempted to seek relief my own way. I might turn to an affair for consolation because I don't believe that God will comfort me.

What we believe about God matters. What we believe affects our desires and, therefore, our choices. To break the power of regret, we must know certain solid truths about God. We must dive deep into His Word and study His character to understand how He can soothe our wounds and guide us through difficult times.

When my husband was ill, we saw numerous doctors, and all of them required us to fill out the same medical history forms. Marty was too ill to do it, so the task fell to me. I soon realized that there were a lot of things I didn't know about him. I had four choices: I could assume the best and answer that he hadn't suffered any health problems; I could assume the worst and say that he'd had all kinds of diseases and ailments; I could leave the spaces blank and let the doctor decide what to do about the lack of information; or I could ask Marty and get the right answer. Obviously, the wisest choice was to ask. To do anything else would have placed my husband's already failing health in an even more precarious position.

Often when we struggle with regret, we have large gaps in our knowledge of God. Unfortunately, this often leads to one of two mistakes. We might fill in the blanks with negative, wrongful assumptions about His character and assume that He is uncaring and unwilling to help us ("He didn't heal my mom, so He must not care"). Or, at the sacrifice of peace and passionate faith, we might leave the problem to someone else ("Someday I'll have to ask my pastor why God didn't heal my mom"). Though pastors, mentors, and authors can guide us toward a true understanding of God, we should individually and personally seek an accurate, intimate knowledge of Him.

Like a child would want to know his loving father, so we should desire to know our heavenly Father. When we do, we will begin to realize just how cherished we have been our whole lives. As J. I. Packer says, "We are all loved just as fully as Jesus is loved. It is like a fairy story—the reigning monarch adopts waifs and strays to make princes of them—but, praise God, it is not a fairy story: it is hard and solid fact, founded on the bedrock of free and sovereign grace."[7]

Unfortunately, few Christians are willing to invest the time and energy it takes to know their own Father. Passiveness is a poison we willingly drink, and it's killing us spiritually. If we will choose to know our Father intimately, we will have more than enough of our questions answered to enable us to avoid not only faux pearls and faux pas, but also persistent regret.

PEARLS OF GREAT PRICE

The more I came to know God, the more equipped and strengthened I became to move past my past. The more I came to know Him, the more I realized the liberating power of two fundamental truths about Him:

God is always good.

God is sovereign all the time.

Perhaps these ideas are not new to you. You may have already come across them in sermons and books. But have you grappled with them enough to become convinced that they are utterly true?

Many Scriptures speak of God's goodness. "The goodness of God endureth continually" (Psalm 52:1, KJV). Speaking of the Father, the psalmist says, "You are good, and what you do is good" (Psalm 119:68). The Bible is also filled with proclamations that God is firmly in control of His creation. "Our God is in heaven; he does whatever pleases him" (Psalm 115:3). Daniel 4:35 declares, "All the peoples of the earth are regarded as nothing. He does as he pleases with the powers of heaven and the peoples of the earth. No one can hold back his hand or say to him: 'What have you done?'" The Bible is clear: God is always good, and He's always in control.

If we suffer losses that seem unjust or senseless, it can be hard to accept the truth of God's goodness; if we are wracked by regret, it can be hard to accept the truth of God's sovereignty. Thankfully, neither our circumstances nor our doubts can change these truths.

Once I had grasped them, my searching turned from questions about me and my failings to questions about God's sovereignty and His will for my life. When that happened, regret was on its way to becoming a thing of the past. What questions about God did I wrestle with? What were my conclusions, and how did they bring about inner peace in my heart? As I look back, four stand out in my mind.

1. Is God's Will Completely Revealed?

I had been taught that God's will can be found in Scriptures that tell us to "do this, and do that, but for goodness sake don't do *that*." When I am focused on a major decision, trying to reach a goal, or dealing with temptation, that teaching helps me. But when it came to overcoming regret, it kept me stuck because, according to this interpretation, I had already acted outside of God's will. The implication was that I could ruin God's plans. So I asked, "Is God's will completely revealed?" I wanted to know—in light of God's sovereignty—if His will is encompassed only in His holy standard, His law.

Isaiah 53:10 says this about the crucifixion of Christ: "Yet it was the LORD's will to crush him and cause him to suffer." Jesus didn't crucify Himself; men crucified Him. Or did they? Well, yes, they did, but they committed the sin of crucifying Jesus within the context of God's will. John Piper writes: "His purposes encompass all things, including sin. Thus the crucifixion of Christ was the will of God, even though it was the greatest sin ever committed."[8] For some mysterious reason, man's sinful choices are encompassed in the secret will of God. If the Jews of Jesus' time sinned within the parameters of God's will, then it seemed to me that God's sovereignty covered my sin as well. I became a little freer from regret when I began to believe that I had not frustrated God's purposes.

2. Does God's Will Change?

I had also been taught that God's will is always changing based on my decisions. I was told that God had a plan A for my life, but when I messed that up with bad choices, He presented me another viable plan—plan B. While that teaching gave me a measure of comfort (since God would always have a purpose for me), it also kept me mired in regret because I continually wondered what God's plan A had been. And I longed to somehow get back to that "best" plan. So I asked, "Does God's will change?"

This question was important because although Jesus was crucified according to the will of God, I needed to know if His crucifixion was plan A or plan B. What I learned is summed up in two words from Ephesians 3:11: "according to his eternal purpose which he accomplished in Christ Jesus our Lord." *Eternal purpose.* His plan has never changed. God's sovereignty cannot be disconnected from His other attributes. Therefore, God is, has always been, and will always be immutably sovereign (permanently in control), omniscient (all-knowing), and omnipotent (all-powerful). He knows everything, and He has the power to do what He wants about what He knows. R. C. Sproul says this about God's will:

> Omnipotence contains the idea that God has all power and
> authority over his creation, including the actions of human
> beings. Whatever God knows will happen, he knows he

can prevent from happening.... If, for example, God knows I will choose to sin, he has the power to annihilate me in an instant to keep me from sinning. If he chooses not to destroy me but to "let" me sin, he chooses to do so. Insofar as he knows it and permits it, it is within the scope of his will that I do it.[9]

The conclusion I came to is that God is unchangeable and, therefore, so is His will. I became even freer of regret when I realized that God's will is not determined by, or subject to, my choices.

3. When Did God Establish His Will for Me?

Another thing I had been taught regarding God's will was this: Because God is sovereign, there is only one plan (plan A) for my life, but that plan is based on His divine foreknowledge of my choices. In other words, according to this teaching, what I am living is not necessarily God's original, best intent for me, but possibly the one He settled for based on the choices He knew I would make before I made them.

That teaching gave me some assurance that I hadn't surprised God with my failures, but it kept me stuck in regret because it suggested that my life *could* have been better *if only* I had made better choices. I wanted the plan-A life I could have had if only I hadn't made so many consequential mistakes (which God knew I would make).

When I read Ephesians 2:10, the questions started coming. That verse says, "For we are God's workmanship, created in Christ Jesus to do good works, which God prepared in advance for us to do." Did God prepare those good works for me before or after my bad choices? He either created me with a purpose, saw what choices I would make, and then adjusted His plans accordingly—or He determined to create me without a specific purpose and then decided my purpose *after* foreseeing my choices. My question was, "When did God establish His will for me?"

I didn't have to search far for an answer because I had already learned that God's nature is *eternally* unchangeable. While the plan A/plan B view of God's will suggested that His will was changing in *time,* what I had learned about God's foreknowledge suggested that His will changed, but that it did so in eternity, before He created me. It seemed logical to apply God's unchangeable nature to eternity.

Martin Luther explained the relationship between God's sovereignty and His will this way:

> Do you suppose that He does not will what He foreknows, or that He does not foreknow what He wills? If He wills what He foreknows, His will is eternal and changeless, because His nature is so. From which it follows, by resistless logic, that all we do, however it may appear to us to be done mutably and contingently, is in reality done necessarily and immutably in respect of God's will. For the will of God is effective and cannot be impeded, since power belongs to God's nature; and His wisdom is such that He cannot be deceived. Since, then, His will is not impeded, what is done cannot but be done where, when, how, as far as, and by whom, He foresees and wills.[10]

In essence what Luther is saying is that God doesn't just will because He foreknows; He foreknows *because* He wills. That is, because God's will is unchangeable, His *foreknowledge* means more than *foreseeing*. This meant that God's will was never—not now, nor in eternity past—determined by my choices. I took a huge step in overcoming my regret when I understood that God sovereignly created me and equipped me for specific, preplanned good works. He has not settled for some good works based on my choices.

4. Which Has the Final Say, God's Sovereignty or My Freedom to Make Choices?

This question has inspired a centuries-old controversy and volumes of material from the most brilliant minds in Christendom.[11] We must acknowledge that, this side of heaven, we will never know all of the answers to questions as profound as this. Obviously, God didn't intend us to, for if we had all the answers, faith wouldn't be necessary. We are called to trust God when we don't understand, and, as in the case of this question, to acknowledge that we do not fully understand.

Nevertheless, it is vital that Christians know what they believe about God's sovereignty and man's will. In *Willing to Believe,* R. C. Sproul tells us why this is so:

> How we understand the will of man…touches heavily on our view of our humanity and God's character. The age-old debate between Pelagianism and Augustinianism is played out in the arena of these issues. Any view of the human will that destroys the biblical view of human responsibility is seriously defective. Any view of the human will that destroys the biblical view of God's character is even worse. The debate will affect our understanding of God's righteousness, sovereignty and grace. If we ignore these issues

or regard them as trivial, we greatly demean the full character of God as revealed in Scripture."[12]

Understanding what we believe and why we believe it is crucial because, as Sproul says, "At issue is the grace and glory of God."[13]

The answer to this fourth question did not come easily for me. But by answering the first three questions and by studying the character of God in His Word, I came to believe that God's sovereignty has the final say on all matters of His creation. And when I believed *that*, regret became a thing of my past.

GOD'S WILL AND OVERCOMING REGRET

Many Christians take their view of God's will, mix it together with their talents, circumstances, and interests, and come up with what they think is God's plan A for them. When they fail, and their plan becomes impossible, they imagine that there is always plan B (and I suppose C, D, and E). After all, as the saying goes, "God is a God of second chances." This dictum dooms regretful people to wish forever that they could get back God's best—that elusive plan A. Although it is intended to dispel regret, it ends up feeding it.

The good news is that we don't have to stay in that hopeless place. I now believe that because God is sovereign, what we see as plan B (God's adjusted plan for our life, based on our mistakes) is actually His plan A (God's full will in action). I believe that my life *is* plan A, and it is God's best for me, just as it is.

Ultimately, because God is sovereign, God's will is whatever happens. Does that make us less responsible for our actions or get us off the hook when we sin? Absolutely not. Surely we pay a price when we sin. Suffering painful and sometimes permanent consequences for wrongdoing is a reality of life. But no matter what those consequences are, they are also part of God's will and purpose for our lives. God doesn't tell us fully what His purposes are, but because *He* is good, *His purposes* are good.

The Westminster Shorter Catechism says: "The chief end of man is to glorify God and enjoy Him forever." Author John Piper has modified it to read: "The chief end of God is to glorify God and enjoy himself forever."[14] While we are on earth, we will never fully understand how He does that and why His love encompasses us in bringing it about. But in the end, we don't need to know *why* things are as they are or what purpose our regrets serve; we just need to trust that God is, indeed, in charge of all things.

CULTURED PEARLS

The only difference between a cultured pearl and a natural one is this: Instead of nature putting an irritant in the oyster, causing it to form a pearl, man puts the irritant in place. Either way, the result is a pearl, but the cultured pearl is much less valuable. The same is true of cultured pearls of truth, which place man at the center. The most valuable pearls of truth will always have God at the center. They will begin from God, be experienced through God, and ultimately bring glory to God and God alone.

The sovereignty of God is a truth that is often falsely presented as a cultured pearl—a pearl because God *is* sovereign, but cultured (and therefore less valuable) because it makes God's will subservient to our own. When we believe that our choices have circumvented

God's sovereign will (e.g., "My divorce has messed up God's original plan"), we have put ourselves at the center of truth—a place that belongs only to God.

Basically, I was *taught* to regret, taught to feel worldly sorrow. God's sovereignty was presented to me in such a way that applying it left me in pain. But the truth has set me free. Jesus said that not one sparrow "will fall to the ground apart from the will of your Father. And even the very hairs of your head are all numbered" (Matthew 10:29–30). What a beautiful way for Jesus to say that God is sovereign and good—in every detail.

Often Christians will say that God is in control but believe that things could have turned out differently "if only." For instance, if a drunk driver kills a mother's teenage daughter, we will say that the girl's life was not cut short, but completed—because God is in control. We will comfort the mother by saying that though we don't understand God's purposes, we know He will use this suffering in her life for His glory—because God is sovereign. But to the drunk driver we will say, "If only you hadn't gotten behind the wheel that night." We may think that we believe God is in control, but when we apply that doctrine to real life, we often find that we really believe just the opposite. The biggest manifestation of my own lack of belief in God's sovereignty was my inability to get over regret.

The misconception that I am somehow the final arbiter of my existence—that "God is in control, but my choices better be right"—has three specific and dangerous consequences.

First, if our decisions have the last word on our existence, then Christians truly can be victims. That teen didn't have to die. Maybe it wasn't her time. But if God is the final word on all matters, then

Christians are not victims—only pilgrims with different sets of luggage to carry on their journey.

Second, if our choices are the bottom line, then there isn't a way to live without the worldly sorrow of regret. It's as simple and as tragic as that. If we believe that our choices can mess up God's will, then we must also believe that we *have* messed up our lives and God's plan—without remedy.

Third (and worst of all), if we believe—either consciously or subconsciously—that we have the final authority through our choices, then we believe that we and the choices we make are more important than God and His purposes. When we do that, we have effectively taken God's entire plan, from before Creation to our gathering at the judgment seat of Christ, and made it all about *us*.

Life, however, is not about us; it's about God. Test the value of your pearl by examining its center carefully. If God is at the center, you have the genuine article. If He is not, toss it back and dive again. Why? Because God has declared, "My glory I will not give to another" (Isaiah 48:11, RSV). And Paul has affirmed, "For from him and through him and to him are all things. To him be the glory for ever" (Romans 11:36, RSV).

BELIEFS MATTER

Maybe you've never considered the relationship between your freedom to choose and God's sovereignty. What I have presented in this chapter is far from a complete study on the will or sovereignty of God. That isn't my purpose here.

Nor is my purpose to convince you that what I believe is right. What you've read may not be what you've been taught; in fact, it may be quite the contrary. If so, remember that Jesus often challenged His followers to examine what they had been taught to discern the truth.

My purpose in examining this question has been to convince you that your theology matters. Asking questions and examining what you believe is one of the most important endeavors in life. It is imperative that you understand for yourself what Scripture teaches because what you believe about God's character permeates every other area of your life. Your understanding of God is also crucial in getting past your past.

But remember, neither your questions nor your regret are ultimately the point. Knowing God is the point. It requires first the right attitude, then the openhearted activity of seeking Him. As you develop a unique relationship with Him and begin to realize His truths, you'll find that they will help you say good-bye to the past you regret.

Once upon a Time

Ending the Fairy Tale

✿ THE LITTLE girl's shoulder-length hair hung in banana curls, much like Shirley Temple's. At times those bouncing ringlets made her feel silly—but not that day. Right then, not even the pronounced sprinkling of freckles on her face, usually despised as blemishes, could bother her. She was lost in a fairy tale.

It was early fall, but as long as the sun was shining, it was still warm enough to roller skate. And what six-year-old in her right mind wouldn't want to? There was nothing like the cool autumn breeze in your face and the steady *clunk, clunk* of skate wheels rolling over cracks in the sidewalk. Caught up in her imaginary world, the girl twirled around in the driveway, pretending to be the most graceful ice skater in the world.

Then she looked up and saw her dad, and suddenly the spell was broken.

He was sitting in his car across the street, obviously ready to go somewhere. For a moment, the girl was torn: Should she ask to go with him or remain in the joy of her daydream? The dilemma didn't last long. Being with Dad was always more fun.

"Daddy, can I go with you?" she called.

His answer was disappointing. "No, honey, not this time."

"Well, where are you going?" the girl asked, hoping at least to find out what she would be missing.

Her dad hesitated and then said, "I'm going to the store. I'll be right back."

That was enough. She paused only long enough to wonder about all the stuff piled in the back of the red Chevrolet, and then she spun on her heel to continue practicing her figure eights.

When her father returned, the car was empty—and it was two weeks later.

That six-year-old girl was me. As I was skating in the driveway that day, my parents decided to end their marriage. My first fairy tale ended, but not with the words "happily ever after." Unfortunately, it didn't end with the word *good-bye,* either. Years later, I could still recall this scene and remember how cheated I felt. Now, of course, I understand. My father's fairy tale was ending too, and saying good-bye was more than he could bear.

RELEASING THE OLD, EMBRACING THE NEW

Endings can be hard to accept, and *good-bye* is often the most difficult word to say, especially if we think it would have been unnecessary—"if only." But learning to say good-bye to the losses that have resulted from our mistakes is imperative if we're going to shed regret.

In our minds we've probably all written the story of our lives the way we think they *should* be. That story is our fairy tale. It always begins with "once upon a time," but when our mistakes prevent the "happily ever after" we expect, we feel cheated and full of regret.

To deal with a disappointing ending, we must let go of how we think our life "should" be. We must first change our minds and then change our stories—letting go of our will and our preconceived idea of God's will for our lives. We need to say good-bye to what is gone—a marriage or a job or a career—*and* to the dreams that accompanied those losses. When Robert and I divorced in 1987, I had to grieve the loss of my marriage *and* the loss of my dream of being married "until death do us part." In other words, I had to grieve what I'd actually lost and all the dreams that went with it.

Though it will be painful to do, there is a good *reason* to end your "once upon a time" story and a good *way* to do it. We'll discuss how to do it in another chapter. For now, let's focus on why to do it. We need a good reason to enable us to face the pain of letting go of our losses and moving past our past to a constructive life.

The *reason* to end our fairy tale is that *God has a purpose for our life exactly as it is—consequences and all.* To passionately pursue that purpose, we must be living in reality, not fantasy. Saying good-bye to *our* plans is another step to realizing *God's* plan for our life. As A. W. Pink says, "Our disappointments are but His appointments."[1]

How can we believe that God has a purpose for our life *exactly* as it is? By believing the truths we discussed in the last chapter—that God is completely sovereign and thoroughly good, no matter what the circumstances. Ending a fairy tale requires faith that God is in control and "too wise to err and too loving to cause His child a needless tear."[2] Our pain is never for nothing—even the pain caused by our own poor choices.

Believing that God is at work in our life *on purpose* and *for a purpose* gives us a good reason to say good-bye to our fantasy. God's plans are always designed to bring about the best for us. "'For I know the plans I have for you,' declares the LORD, 'plans to prosper you and not to harm you, plans to give you hope and a future'" (Jeremiah 29:11). God said this to the Israelites after they had been carried off into exile in Babylon—an exile God allowed for their good. He told them to grow and prosper in exile because, in time, when the rest of His plan had been fulfilled, the Israelites needed to be ready (see Jeremiah 29:1–14). God planned to return them to the Promised Land—the place He had chosen for them and where they were *sure* God wanted them to be.

God did indeed want His people to have the land He had promised them, but there was a lot of work to be done in their hearts before they could live there as He intended. The Israelites needed to lose the land in order to learn that they could do *nothing* without God. They needed to understand their weakness before they could appreciate God's strength. When they learned that, the Lord would take them back to Israel. *Things would not be as they were, but they would be as God intended.* Through the Israelites' failure, God exposed their pride; through their restoration, He revealed His grace. Through it all, His will was accomplished.

If you feel as if you've been exiled from your promised land, you need to say good-bye to *where you were* and accept *where you are*—not as cruel punishment, but as needed discipline from God to train and prepare you for what lies ahead. The enemy of that bright future is regret. It keeps us pining for the fabled past and prevents us from learning and growing in our exile. It hinders us from passionately pursuing our present and properly preparing for our future—a future that includes "good works, which God prepared in advance for us to do" (Ephesians 2:10).

FACTS AND FABLES

Who doesn't like a good fairy tale? Every prince charming finds his lovely maiden, and they live in eternal bliss, while the evil witch/stepmother/troll is justly punished. Everything is nice and neat with no loose ends or rough edges. Throw in a rainbow with a pot of gold, and the whole package is tied up with a pretty bow.

Unfortunately, real life isn't a fairy tale, is it? In real life, sometimes the princess gets pregnant before the wedding. Sometimes the prince abandons her and takes up with another lover. Sometimes the family in the palace is shattered by a divorce decree. Yes, life is hard and pain inevitable.

When our fairy tales end in disappointment and despair, regret will consume us unless we believe that God's ending to our story, the one He intended all along, will yet come to fruition. The bottom line of our existence is that God started it and that He will finish it—His way. As He clearly states, "My purpose will stand, and I will do all that I please.... What I have said, that will I bring about; what I have planned, that will I do" (Isaiah 46:10–11). God is ruling His creation surely and infinitely. Man doesn't thwart the will of God or frustrate His purposes. Unless we understand this, we will not be able to let go of our regret.

Paul reminds us: "We know that God causes all things to work together for good, to those who love God, to those who are called according to His purpose" (Romans 8:28, NASB). This verse is often used to comfort those with regrets, those who have been mistreated, or those who have experienced tragic loss. However, the well-intentioned people who quote it frequently present it as if it were some sort of consolation prize for those who didn't win big in life. They say something like this: "I know you're suffering terribly, but don't worry. Remember Romans 8:28." (Then they quote the verse.) "See? God will find *some* way to bring good from this." The implication is that God, who didn't or wouldn't intervene to prevent tragedy, will now jump in and *somehow* manage to bring good from calamity.

I don't believe God "manages" man's mistakes. He doesn't scramble around to bring satisfactory results from sin. What does He do? He executes His plan "according to His purpose." *All* of our circumstances, situations, and sufferings are in service to God because He is sovereign.

God will redeem everything that He allows to come into the lives of His children. That is the promise of Romans 8:28. Peace comes from knowing that what He allows is always according to His sovereign wisdom. Our task is not to understand God's purpose, but to trust Him. Dr. Larry Crabb says, "There is no escape in this life from pain and problems.... More than anything else, [we] need a *person to trust,* someone who can give [us] hope, joy, and peace in the midst of life's unpredictable struggles.... A *plan to follow* is not enough."[3]

When we fail to live according to God's standard, and all of our best-laid plans go awry, we must trust that the God we know is far greater than our failures and our regrets. We will be able to accept the ending of our fairy tales when we realize that life isn't out of control, it's just out of *our* control. Once we know that, we can believe that every ending ushers in a new beginning.

So what are God's purposes in allowing us to fail and suffer consequences? Though He may make us wait for total understanding, He doesn't make us wait for an answer.

Our Creator and Re-Creator

Romans 8:29 says, "For those God foreknew he also predestined to be conformed to the likeness of his Son, that he might be the first-born among many brothers." *That* is God's intention for you and me as we battle through life. He is sanctifying us. Sanctification is the progressive "setting apart" of our beings for Christ's use and glory. That setting apart began before the foundation of the earth (Ephesians 1:4), manifested itself at salvation, and continues throughout our lives as God trains us in righteousness. The goal of that training is to shape us into truer likenesses of Jesus Christ—to conform us into His image.

What does that look like? Perfection, of course. Hebrews 4:15 says, "For we do not have a high priest who is unable to sympathize with our weaknesses, but we have one who has been tempted in every way, just as we are—yet was without sin." But that's not all. Hebrews 5:8 adds, "Although he was a son, he learned obedience from what he suffered and, once made perfect, he became the source of eternal salvation for all who obey him." Jesus wasn't *just* perfect; He was *completely* perfect because He remained sinless even in suffering.

God has a work to do *in* us, and He has a work to do *through* us. Salvation may get us off the hook for our sin, but it puts us on the anvil to be formed into the image of Christ. As painful as that is sometimes, it's still an incomprehensible privilege.

Part of the way God forms us is by teaching us that apart from Him we can do nothing (John 15:5). After we discover that, the Lord does a work through us, and we learn that we "can do everything through him who gives [us] strength" (Philippians 4:13). The process of growing spiritually teaches us those two things: Alone we can do nothing, and with Christ we can do everything.

This slow reshaping of our characters—through struggle, failure, and pain—slays the pride that so easily grows in our hearts. Pride is a self-centered perception that life is about *us*, whereas humility is knowing it's not. Knowing that life isn't about us, but about God, is evidence of the Holy Spirit's work in our heart. The holiest people in the world are also the most humble. Understanding their weakness makes them humble, and knowing God's strength makes them mature. Our failure and restoration bring about this maturity. Realizing this puts our own personal tale of woe in eternal perspective.

Because God's goal is to make us perfect just as Jesus is perfect, He will continue the work of reforming our characters as long as we're on earth. But until we reach heaven and totally leave behind our sinful natures, we will sin, and we will suffer consequences and shame. Nevertheless, none of our pain will be wasted—God will use it as part of His purpose. Because He is thoroughly good, that purpose will always be for our good, the good of others, and ultimately for His glory. This truth "clicked" in my brain as I read a prayer from a devotional book:

> I choose to thank You for my weaknesses, my infirmities, my inadequacies (physical, mental, emotional, relational)...for the ways I fall short of what people view as ideal...for my feelings of helplessness and inferiority, and even my pain and distresses. What a comfort it is to know that...in Your infinite wisdom You have allowed these in my life so that they may contribute to Your high purposes for me.
>
> Thank You that I can trust You to remove or change any of my weaknesses and handicaps and shortcomings the moment they are no longer needed for Your glory, and for my good, and for the good of other people.[4]

Nothing is part of my life unless God has allowed it—not even my own weaknesses.

So what is *our* role in being conformed to the likeness of Christ? Romans 8:29 just says that God predestined us *to be* conformed; it doesn't say who does the conforming. Let's look at another Scripture. In his letter to the believers at Philippi, Paul said: "Therefore, my dear friends, as you have always obeyed—not only in my presence, but now much more in my absence—continue to work out your salvation with fear and trembling, *for it is God who works in you to will and to act according to his good purpose*" (Philippians 2:12–13, emphasis added). To the church at Thessalonica he wrote: "May *God himself,* the God of peace, *sanctify you* through and through. May your whole spirit, soul and body be kept blameless at the coming of our Lord Jesus Christ. The one who calls you is faithful and he will do it" (1 Thessalonians 5:23–24, emphasis added).

God is the Creator and the Re-creator. Just as He formed us in His own image from the dust, so He conforms us back to that image from the ashes of our smoldering, ravaged lives. God did the work of salvation, and He does the work of sanctification. The psalmist said, "I will run the way of thy commandments, when thou shalt enlarge my heart" (Psalm 119:32, KJV). The phrase "enlarge my heart" can also be translated "increase my understanding." Through His Spirit, He increases our understanding and gives us strength to obey Him. "And the God of all grace, who called you to his eternal glory in Christ, after you have suffered a little while, will himself restore you and make you strong, firm and steadfast" (1 Peter 5:10).

So why not just throw up our hands and shrug our shoulders in defeat when life becomes difficult? Why strive to obey if the strength to do so comes from God? Let me give you three reasons:

1. We strive to obey through prayer, study, and discipline because that is God's plan for us. They are His divinely chosen tools for the work He's doing in and through us. He teaches and strengthens us through those things. We are responsible to be teachable, to submit ourselves to God, and to actively resist temptation (James 4:7).

2. We strive to obey because the Lord said we are to "work out [our] salvation with fear and trembling" (Philippians 2:12). *We are responsible for what we do,* and we suffer painful consequences when we fail. I don't know about you, but that definitely inspires fear and trembling in me.

God will work in us. We are to be willing to work it out. That requires prayer, study, discipline, fellowship, and perseverance. James 4:8 says, "Come near to God and he will come near to you. Wash your hands, you sinners, and purify your hearts, you double-minded." If we choose a cavalier or defeated attitude toward obedience to Christ, we are being double-minded. Understanding God's sovereignty and our weakness apart from Christ is meant to give us freedom—not a license to disobey.

3. We strive to obey because we will find blessing and prosperity in fulfilling our purpose *only* by doing what God says. James 1:25 says, "But the man who looks intently into the perfect law that gives freedom, and continues to do this, not forgetting what he has heard, but doing it—he will be blessed in what he does." And only when we obey God will we be able to do the good works He has prepared for us. And with those good works will come joy and freedom. Galatians 5:13 says, "You, my brothers, were called to be free. But do not use your freedom to indulge the sinful nature; rather, serve one another in love."

The more we strive to obey God, the more we will grow and be transformed into Christ's image. Perhaps the painful process of overcoming your regret is part of the reshaping God is doing in you. Though that transformation is often difficult, we can be assured that God is completing His purpose in our lives. As that purpose is fulfilled, God's character is revealed and His name glorified—and *that* is the bottom line. As A. W. Pink reminds us in *The Sovereignty of God*:

The Lord God omnipotent reigneth. His government is exercised over inanimate matter, over the brute beasts, over the children of men, over angels good and evil, and over Satan himself. No revolving of the world, no shining of a star, no storm, no movement of a creature, no actions of men, no errands of angels, no deeds of the Devil—*nothing in all the vast universe can come to pass otherwise than God has eternally purposed.* Here is the foundation for faith. Here is a resting place for the intellect. Here is an anchor for the soul, both sure and steadfast. It is not blind fate, unbridled evil, man or Devil, but the Lord Almighty who is ruling the world, ruling it according to His own good pleasure and for His own eternal glory.[5]

ANOTHER STORY, PLEASE

In *The 77 Habits of Highly Ineffective Christians,* Chris Fabry, with his ironic brand of humor, writes: "The past can never come again, so you must bring it back with your mind. Wallow in it. Suck the marrow from the past in your mind, and your eyes will be so glazed that you will not be able to perceive the gift God gives you in the present."[6]

Do you, like most people with regrets, live in the past—without perceiving God's gift in the present? That's what eternal life is: the never-ending present. It doesn't begin when we die; it begins when we're born again. Clinging to our old fairy tale prevents us from seeing how our eternal life is unfolding today, while we are on earth.

Author and speaker Gerard Smith recently told me that he uses the following phrase when speaking to groups about realizing their dreams: "Those who live in the past die in the past." How true. If we are living in the past, living in the here and now has ended for us. We are meant to live life, not just survive it.

Those of us who have ever read a book to a small child know that when we finish one story, we will hear these words: "Another story, *pleeeeze?*" When our fairy tale has ended, that's what we need to do—ask our Father for another story, a new dream, a new direction for our future. Not a plan B, but the ability to see *His* plan A. We need to believe that God can take our old dreams and give us new, better ones. A far superior ending can replace the imagined conclusion to the fairy tale we grieved. Getting past the past involves looking to the future, "forgetting what is behind and straining toward what is ahead" (Philippians 3:13).

But to have a new dream, you must end your fairy tale, and in order to do that, you will have to make a decision. Do you really *want* a new story? Or do you want to keep hearing the same one over and over?

When my youngest child, Michael, was an infant, I was tormented by regret. In my mind, I would constantly replay my life. Each time, I would rewrite the ending to be better than what I was living, and I'd end my fantasy with the words, "Oh, if only…." I'll never forget the day the Lord spoke to me through my baby's cry.

Michael was crying because he was hungry. No problem—I had what he needed. But Michael began sucking so hard and frantically on his pacifier that I couldn't get it out of his mouth to feed him. He could see the milk, and I could see his tortured look. Still, I literally had to wait for him to start crying in frustration before I could remove the pacifier from his mouth. It was as I spoke to my child, telling him to release his pacifier so I could give him what he needed, that God spoke to me with the same message.

Sometimes we don't want to let go of our old dreams because we receive some pleasure from fantasizing about what might have been. Like a pacifier in a baby's mouth, rehearsing the fairy tale offers us a measure of relief. We're afraid that if we let go, there might not be anything to replace it. Letting our old dream die requires faith that God will give us a new one. To receive the life-giving change our hungry souls cry for, we must release our pacifiers. God is patient. He will wait for us to cry in frustration if necessary. He will wait for us to stop saying "if only" and start saying "what now?"

I recall one particular dream that was hard for me to give up. In 1990, I was attending a Bible study that had certain rules regarding people in leadership. One of those rules was that no divorced person could be a leader. I very much wanted to be a leader, and for a long time I struggled with thinking, *If only I weren't divorced.* It wasn't until the day I saw my son working so hard on his pacifier that I realized that I needed to release my own. When I let go of my "if only," God opened my eyes to other possibilities and gave me a dream and purpose far beyond what I ever hoped or imagined— the dream and purpose of writing.

Dreaming is simply envisioning what your purpose might be. Without a new and exciting dream—one that propels us forward— we end up stuck in place, standing still, stagnating. If that's your aim, then here's more tongue-in-cheek advice from Chris Fabry:

> To be ineffective, you must strive for stagnant living. One of the best ways to accomplish this is to quell all efforts at "the dream."
>
> I define "the dream" as your God-given, nagging sense

of purpose…. "The dream" keeps coming back to you, as if God were pushing you toward an ultimate goal…. You must fight these little whispers from the Almighty.[7]

If the word *mediocrity* has a nice ring to it, then by all means keep squelching your dream. Just keep looking back at all those dreams that never materialized and avoid envisioning what great things God has in store for you. If, on the other hand, you're eager to get past your past and get on with the future, take hold of a new dream.

But what if you don't perceive a new dream? Isaiah 43:18–19 says, "Forget the former things; do not dwell on the past. See, I am doing a new thing! Now it springs up; do you not perceive it? I am making a way in the desert and streams in the wasteland." The implication of this verse is that some people have trouble seeing the "new thing" God is doing. If you cannot perceive the new dream God has designed for you, try spending time with people who might see what you don't. Often when we can't see what makes us special, others can. Serving our purpose will always include serving people. Get involved. See the needs, and you'll begin to see "the dream."

As you seek insight about how God might use you, consider these wise words from neurosurgeon Ben Carson, who has accomplished great things despite growing up in less than ideal circumstances:

- Listen to those who have already achieved, and think you can do likewise.
- Understand that achievement does not just happen to a few, selected people.

- Take advantage of the opportunities to learn from any source that can teach you.
- Learn from the mistakes (as well as achievements) of others.[8]

When you begin to think about your future, think big—*dream huge*—but don't think only in terms of tangible things, such as a spouse, family, career, or ministry. Dream also of the more important, intangible things of God. Dream of spiritual maturity. Look ahead, dream anew, but never forget that we're seeking to serve God and fulfill *His* purposes, not our own. If we seek God's purposes, it's more likely that His plan will become our dream and that our dream will then come true—all to His glory.

A Real "Happily Ever After"

If you struggle with regret, you know some of the hard realities of life. One of them is that even when things are going well, even when you overcome regret, life on earth still leaves us longing for more. Our lives here are never quite satisfying.

God intended it to be that way. Why? Because there is a place we hope for and dream about that is *not* a fairy tale. No more sad good-byes. No more bad endings. It's the place our Father has promised to His children as an inheritance, the place where everything we desire and yearn for will be given to us. God doesn't want us to forget that "our citizenship is in heaven. And we eagerly await a Savior from there, the Lord Jesus Christ" (Philippians 3:20). Our lives here are a journey homeward. When we get there, we'll sigh, "Ah, home at last." Finally, we'll be free from even the *presence* of sin. Finally, all will be right. No time, no space, no pain, no regret—only love and worship and freedom.

Until then, God wants us to focus on His kingdom. When we do, He graciously gives us a portion of it here and now, in time and space, by doing His sanctifying work in us and then using us to lead others to the kingdom. This is God's will, as Jesus prayed in Matthew 6:10: "Your kingdom come, your will be done on earth as it is in heaven."

When we set our eyes on God's purposes for His kingdom, Jesus becomes our Prince of Peace in the present and turns our hearts toward the future, toward eternal life—the true "happily ever after."

10

Refugees of Regret

Fleeing a Hopeless Past

WHEN I was a child, the Vietnam War was on the news every night—in vivid color. Along with the shocking film of combat were images of thousands of desperate refugees who took to the sea to flee the devastation, danger, and persecution. Many of these "boat people" set out from the beaches at night, hoping the darkness would protect them from the communist government that threatened to destroy them.

Their voyages were frightening. Large numbers of people crowded into small dinghies with few provisions. Most had paid enormous amounts of money for their beat-up little boats. Some had given up all they had for the chance to be free. The very old, the very young, pregnant and nursing women, and the disabled all huddled together in uncertainty. The only thing they were sure of was that if they were going to survive, they *had* to leave; despite their fear and grief, they had to say good-bye forever to what lay behind them.

An Tran's family lived what I watched on the news. An Tran himself was fortunate. His wife's brother-in-law was a U.S. citizen, so An and his immediate family were able to leave Vietnam by plane. His brother and four sisters and their families were not so fortunate. Among the huddled masses I saw tossed about on the sea on my television screen were An's sister Sarah, her husband, Tinh, and their children. This was a family of Christians in a country being overtaken by communism. Being Christians gave them more reason to leave, but their faith also gave them the strength and courage to take the risk. Tinh later told their story.[1]

Tinh says, "Between 1976 and 1978, I had made one official attempt to leave and nine unofficial ones." He then goes on to give what could be the story line from a scary and heart-wrenching movie. The plot included lies, extortion, abuse, thwarted plans, dashed hopes, and endless fear. Tinh and Sarah Phan were so afraid to stay in Vietnam that they actually tried to negotiate for various members of their family to leave Vietnam *individually*. So great was the risk to their lives that Tinh and Sarah were willing to separate from their children and send them out alone into an unpredictable future.

For a long time every effort to leave failed. Tinh says, "Each attempt—nine in all—resulted in failure. And each time, I lost money because deposits were never returned and there was no one to whom I could complain."

The ninth attempt to leave was the most terrifying. Tinh had been carefully, and of course secretly, negotiating with a fisherman who had a boat. Tinh not only agreed to pay a large sum of money for his family to travel, but he also agreed to finance the entire escape. He paid more than twenty-five thousand dollars for him and his family to ride in a flimsy fishing boat to an unknown destination. "But it looked like the plan was going to succeed, so I really wasn't counting the cost," Tinh recalled. "To leave was worth anything—even everything, if need be."

So under the cover of night, the family made a risky, two-hundred-mile bus trip up the coast. They arrived at the seaport only to discover that the fisherman they had hired had been gripped by fear and refused to go. Devastated, Tinh and Sarah returned home, "right where we started—and much poorer."

Finally, after masquerading as Chinese, being strip-searched, paying nearly seventy-five thousand dollars more, giving up all their valuables except three hundred dollars in cash and five ounces of gold, they left the only country they had ever known. Tinh, Sarah, and their children, along with a hundred other people, boarded a forty-five by eleven-foot fishing boat destined for anywhere outside of Vietnam. Tinh says, "After prayer together, we plunged into the uncertain future with never a backward glance."

The boat they were on had two decks. When the boat was used for fishing, the purpose of the lower level was to store the day's catch—and it smelled like it. That's where Sarah and Tinh spent the next two and half days, eating nothing but oranges, drinking dirty river water, and along with every other man, woman, and child on board, vomiting from the repulsive smell, rolling waves, and constant fear.

Finally, a Malaysian patrol boat spied the floundering vessel and ordered it, along with other refugee boats, to follow a police boat to shore. Land and relief were in sight. But the boat transporting Tinh's family couldn't keep up. Tinh recalls:

In a short while, the engine stopped and our boat was left behind, apparently unnoticed, wallowing in the swells. I think we were about five miles from land at the time. It was too deep to anchor, and although we signaled many fishing boats and commercial ships which came close, no one stopped to give aid.

Pounded by the waves and without engine power, the boat started to leak and for the next twenty-four hours, I was sure we would perish within sight of land. Fear tormented me. We were the only Christians on board, and we sang and prayed. We also cried and repented because we were sure it was the end. My nine-year-old Bich Son took my hand and smiled weakly. It was too much. I thought, *What have I done to them? God, forgive me.*

Finally, another Malaysian police boat came along and towed the vessel to calmer waters at the mouth of a river. There, the men were allowed to get out of the boat to find food and water for the women and children. They stayed there four more days, until another fishing boat picked them up and took them to a refugee camp on an island twenty miles off the Malaysian coast.

The Phan family had done it. Though it had cost them dearly, and the refugee camp would present horrible challenges of its own, they had nonetheless escaped their disappointing and hopeless past.

EMOTIONAL REFUGEES

I include this harrowing story because there are striking parallels between refugees who flee one country for another and emotional "refugees of regret." To gain freedom and arrive on a new shore brimming with possibilities, people who struggle with regret must choose to leave the place of failure and remorse and embark on a difficult journey through grief and healing.

In the previous chapter I said that it is important to say good-bye to what we've lost and let go of how we had *hoped* the story of our life would read. If we don't acknowledge our losses, there is no emotional resolution to our regret, and without resolution, we remain resident in our past, unable to see the promise of our future.

Often we won't say good-bye because doing so brings fear and grief that we would rather avoid. For years that was my problem. Instead of facing my losses, I stayed on the shore of regret, hoping that staying in the past was still an option. Like Tinh and Sarah, I needed to see that holding on to my past was more dangerous than facing, with desperate hope, an unknown future.

In order to put my past and regret behind me, I needed to face the same reality they did: My past was hopeless. I needed to see that my only hope of finding a new land of dreams and purpose was to make the hard journey of acknowledging and then accepting my losses. For me, that sometimes meant feeling like an emotional refugee. At times I have felt as if I were floundering in a sea of unpredictable emotions, where the pain was so deep that I thought I would drown.

Why a Refugee?

When you trust that God is sovereign and good, loss is not necessarily devastating. I mentioned that my husband, Marty, was diagnosed with cancer when my three children were all under age ten. He and my mom were diagnosed with cancer four weeks apart and died five weeks apart. Needless to say, that was an extremely difficult and painful time. But because I truly believed that God was sovereign and good, it was not a hopeless time. My grief was deep, but even so I did not despair.

There were other times, however, when I faced loss that could be considered far less significant, yet I was absolutely consumed by the pain. Those were times when I was acknowledging losses that stemmed from my own failures. Because of my poor choices in high school, I lost my innocence and an opportunity for an education. Because of my divorce in my early twenties, I lost the chance to see my daughter grow up in the same house with her father, and I lost my dream of the white picket fence and "happily ever after."

The difference between the losses—those I could endure and those that shook me to my core—was determined by my belief in God's goodness and sovereignty. In one instance, I really believed the truth. In the other, I was surprised to find that I really didn't. God's sovereignty can be hard to believe when you are faced with pain you have brought on yourself.

The prophet Jeremiah said, "The heart is more deceitful than all else and is desperately sick; who can understand it?" (Jeremiah 17:9, NASB). My deceitful heart had deceived my feelings as well as my weak faith, so when I finally acknowledged my losses, I experienced a devastating grief. I was in greater pain when I was grieving the losses caused by choices I regretted than I was when my husband and mother were dying.

After I applied the truth to my feelings, it took some time for the pain to subside. In the meantime, my regret brought grief, and my grief brought more regret. Faith got harder, feelings got more intense, and I felt much like a refugee in a boat on the open sea.

If we trust in God's sovereignty and goodness during times of loss, then grief may not last long or cause despair. Without trust, grief will likely be prolonged and cause depression. Until we convince ourselves that God's truth applies to the particular loss we are grieving, we will probably feel like emotional refugees.

The Need to Flee

Getting in a boat isn't something any refugee *wants* to do. Refugees get into boats because they fear they will die if they don't. They know they must move forward. There is fear that the journey may bring terrible hardship, perhaps even death—but there is also the saving thought, *Imagine the possibilities if I survive!*

For me, one of the most difficult aspects of my journey from regret was taking that first step into the boat—acknowledging my losses. I didn't want to acknowledge them because I didn't want them to be true. Only when my need to move forward was greater than my fear of pain did I finally take the step—but once I did, I was able to begin to apply the truth to my damaged emotions. That was a difficult process, but if I hadn't gone through it, I would not have been able to get fully past my past. Acceptance of loss isn't optional; it's a matter of emotional survival.

Stepping into the boat meant trading familiar ground for the murky unknown. It meant letting go of my sometimes comforting "if onlys." I pushed off into a stormy sea of uncertainty, where tides of emotion and confusion seemed to keep me drifting aimlessly. For a long time, I felt like I couldn't go back, but I couldn't go forward, either.

Moving Forward—In Circles

Grief is one of those great paradoxes of life. In weakness, we get stronger; in feeling broken, we are made whole; in being confused, we find clarity. It is an emotionally chaotic time. We can feel much like Tinh and Sarah did—fearful, yet courageous; desperate, yet optimistic; distressed, yet hopeful.

Like refugees, we're in limbo, and we feel much like we're doing the dance of the same name—we're walking forward while leaning back. It's not a comfortable position, and it's hard to see where we're going. We want to hurry through the pain, but rushing this dance means we'll most certainly fall. Each step must be taken deliberately and carefully, despite the discomfort. My journal entries reflected my struggle to continue the dance, despite the pain:

> My spirit knows that God is in control, but my heart cries out in pain and wants to grasp what it thinks it needs. When my spirit and my heart agree, there will be comfort. Peace I will grasp now, knowing who is in control and sits enthroned. Comfort I will wait for.

Loss is a peculiar feeling. Although it's something that happened in the past, we experience it in the present. As the past and the future jockey for position in our minds, confusion seems a constant companion. Desperation collides with hope. Fear tangles with healing. Panic challenges determination. But even in those times of jumbled feelings, I knew that acknowledging my losses and applying the truth to my damaged emotions was the way *through* my pain and on to true healing.

The Final Embrace

It is most often in hindsight that we appreciate the value of grieving. Only when we have gone through it, or watched someone close to us emerge from that dark tunnel, can we see what a privilege it is to say good-bye.

When my husband and mother were simultaneously terminally ill, I had a close relationship with grief. When others asked me how I was "doing it," I often thought of those who didn't have the chance to say good-bye.

My cousin Kellie died instantly in a car crash when she was only fifteen. There was no time for good-byes, no final embraces, no treasured last words of love. There was only sudden silence. *That* made me appreciate the time I had with my husband and mother. I was able to say good-bye, embrace one last time, and say one final, "I love you." The only thing more painful than that last good-bye is not having the chance to say it.

It is when we are in the boat on the sea of grief that we embrace what we had for a season and then *release* it. This time is our emotional "final embrace." When we finally release whatever is already gone, we also let go of a large measure of regret. Sometimes we release something tangible, such as a person or a failed business. Other times, we release something intangible, such as a good reputation or a dream. No matter what it is, that final embrace allows us to cherish it for a moment, acknowledge that it is lost, and then let it go.

As difficult as it is to say good-bye, the Holy Spirit enables us to do it. It is the Spirit of God who gives us strength to leave the past, journey through grief, and anticipate a new beginning. The Spirit bolsters our faith in the goodness and sovereignty of God.

No biblical character illustrates this kind of faith more than Job.

In a Pile…and Praising God

There he was—his children dead, his wealth gone, his health in severe jeopardy. Loss upon loss lay stretched out before him. Pain was the uninvited houseguest who wouldn't leave, and Job wanted to know why. God never did tell him, but He did drop in on Job for a visit—one that forever changed Job's point of view.

One of the chapters in Philip Yancey's book *Disappointment with God* is titled "Why Job Died Happy." Yancey observes that many people think Job died happy because he was eventually restored. He had more children; he regained twice his wealth; his health returned. But Yancey argues cogently against that view:

> These readers, however, overlook one important detail: Job spoke his contrite words before any of his losses had been restored. He was still sitting in a pile of rubble, naked, covered with sores, and it was in *those* circumstances that he learned to praise God. Only one thing had changed: God had given Job a glimpse of the big picture.[2]

Job repented, praised His maker, and died happy despite his losses because of two things: He realized that he had no right to demand answers from God, and he applied God's sovereignty and goodness to his situation. He still had no idea why his life had been so shattered. Yet based solely on what he knew of God's character, he chose faith. As Yancey says, "Faith means believing in advance what will only make sense in reverse."[3] That kind of faith turns disappointment with *God* into disappointment with *life*. The latter can be accepted. The former leaves us hopeless because it crumbles the foundation of our existence. If God can't be trusted, who can? Job resolved in his heart that not only is God in complete control, but that He is also completely good, and therefore, trustworthy. When we have settled those things in our heart, we are in a position not only to die happy, but to live happy—despite our circumstances.

JOY COMES IN THE MOURNING

Strength is critical for the survival of any refugee. When I asked An Tran how his family found strength to endure the hardships they suffered, he told me, "The only way they survived their ordeals was through the strength that came from faith in Jesus Christ."

Putting your past behind you and looking forward to the future puts you, for a while, in the sea of grief—somewhere between "if only" and "what now?" I wonder if that's how Jesus' disciples felt on the Saturday after His death. I've often wondered about that Saturday. We know the significance of Good Friday and the glory of Easter Sunday, but what about the day in between? What was it like for the disciples? They had abandoned Jesus in His darkest hour. Although a couple of them had followed at a distance, not one came to His defense. I wonder what the grieving, hopeless, guilt-ridden, and confused disciples were doing between their failure and their future? Spending some time with regret, perhaps?

Since Scripture is silent, we can only speculate.

Regardless, joy and strength would return to the disciples. Their joy would come in the morning because Easter Sunday was on the way. But joy would also come in their *mourning*—their grief was turned to joy the moment they saw the risen Christ. Joy comes whenever and wherever we see Jesus Christ, and joy leads to strength: "The joy of the LORD is your strength" (Nehemiah 8:10).

During the last weeks of my husband's life, I made many hour-long journeys to the hospital alone—trying to divide my time wisely between my ill husband and my needy children. On one of those trips I was doing what I usually did—listening to Christian music, singing along with the radio, and praising God—when I was struck by how *extraordinary* it was to be singing God's praises with gladness while on the way to visit my terminally ill husband.

I began to question myself: *How can I feel this joy? Am I in denial?* I knew I wasn't. I knew that without a miracle Marty was going to die soon. I had even started planning his funeral. I realized that I was praising God because I had studied His Word long enough to *know,* deep in my heart, the truth that He could be trusted. I *knew* and truly *felt* that Marty, my children, and I were safe in His hands. That truth gave me strength to endure my pain.

Suddenly I was overwhelmed with gratitude to God that He had given me strength in the time of my crisis. He had done it by giving me joy. I was also awed by something else. Even the discovery of Him was a joyful experience. What a generous God! It had literally been in the joy of discovery that the discovery of joy had come.

Apart from faith, we can have no real joy—and apart from joy, very little strength. Paul said that God's "power is made perfect in weakness" (2 Corinthians 12:9). I had often wondered how this could be. That day in my car, I understood it a little better.

I receive joy from trusting in *God's* strength—in His character—even while I am experiencing my own weakness or grief. Believing that God is good and in control means I feel safe and loved. And when I feel safe and loved, I feel a joy that is not dependent upon my circumstances. So it is through faith in God that He imparts His joy and, therefore, His strength to me. He gives me "the oil of gladness instead of mourning, and a garment of praise instead of a spirit of despair" (Isaiah 61:3).

Tinh and Sarah's story reminded me of that day in my car. When things were the worst for them, and they feared death the most, they were singing. It is joy in the middle of heartache that gives us the strength to survive.

Besides strength, there is one more key to being a successful refugee: hope. Paul tells us that we aren't to "grieve like the rest of men, who have no hope" (1 Thessalonians 4:13). Our faith in the goodness and sovereignty of God gives us hope that wherever we are going will be better than where we have been. Because God is in control and He is good, we have every reason to hope for a bright future.

PAIN WITH PURPOSE

When we've made a journey through grief and are preparing to step onto a land of hope, we realize something significant: Though permanent loss *does* mean your life is permanently changed, it doesn't mean you will experience permanent pain. I'm sure Job never stopped longing to see the ten children who had died, yet he died happy.

That excites me because it reveals a wonderful truth. The pain associated with regret *can* end! It feels like a miracle to me that I now have to struggle to recall the pain I once thought would kill me. When I do remember it, it's not the same as it used to be. It's like trying to recall the pain of childbirth. I remember that it hurt, but I don't actually feel the suffering anymore.

Part of my healing, like Job's, came from believing that God has a plan that my eyes can't see. Through our failure and loss, God develops in us the faith and character we need to fulfill His objectives for our lives. In other words, pain has a purpose—it strengthens us so we can complete God's plan for us.

I once heard an interview with a woman who has adopted, loved, and lost many children. She said, "I've learned that life is a series of necessary losses, with moments of blessed happiness in between." When we embrace that fact, we can view pain as a temporary, but necessary, visitor in our lives. And though happiness will come and go, joy can remain constant.

But there's more than just surviving the sea, even with joy. There's the hope of what lies ahead. Tinh and Sarah didn't stay in their refugee camp. They settled in Southern California, resumed their careers in the jewelry business, finished raising their family, and then retired—in freedom. The entire Tran family not only survived being refugees, they have thrived. Their family now includes pastors, engineers, and those working in various Christian ministries. They are living testimonies that we can enter the confusing, frightening world of a refugee and arrive safely on a different shore. And now when they tell their encouraging stories, they change lives by giving glory to the One who is responsible for their survival and success.

What about you? When you sail away from regret, how will God use your life to help someone else? When you step out of your boat of grief, what will you contribute to your new land? What stories will *you* live to tell?

11

The Temptations of Lamentations

Three Don'ts and Some Do's of Grief

🌿 ISRAEL HAD blown it.

The nation's repeated sin and rebellion had brought judgment from God and terrible consequences. The Babylonians besieged Jerusalem, destroyed the temple, carried the Israelites into captivity, and left the city desolate.

The book of Lamentations vividly expresses the nation's pain and loss: "Joy is gone from our hearts; our dancing has turned to mourning" (5:15). "Jerusalem remembers all the treasures that were hers in days of old" (1:7). In sin, the Israelites could deny or ignore their spiritual bankruptcy. In pain, reality slapped them in the face. Lamentations is so named because it describes the Israelites lamenting their losses.

Sin caused Israel's loss; loss caused Israel to notice its sin; and grief over the loss brought Israel to repentance and restored blessing. Israel's experience is not unique. We also hurt and lament when we lose something or someone. And like Israel, it is in pain that we are sometimes most willing to repent and grow in faith. God humbles us when we are hurt and feeling helpless.

As I said earlier, accepting the losses incurred by poor choices is crucial to getting past our past because it's only in facing reality that we become content in it. But facing reality is hard and painful, and grieving brings with it unique troubles all its own. So while we are grieving and voicing our own lamentations, we must avoid three major temptations—the redo, the undo, and the don't do.

THE REDO

Many years ago, I worked with Yvonne, who had an on-again, off-again affair with a married man. It was an intermittent relationship because Yvonne's feelings were sporadic. Her conscience would cause her to feel miserable, so she would break off the relationship. Then feelings of loss and guilt for hurting her lover would overwhelm her, so she would justify resuming the affair.

Yvonne knew it was a dead-end relationship. She knew it was wrong. But her pain overruled her conscience time after time. Inevitably, the constant redoing of the relationship caused Yvonne more grief than if she had endured the original pain of terminating the relationship. I'll never forget how she described her grief as she became more and more attached to a man she couldn't have: "I'm sad that we started what we can't finish; sad that we started what we must finish; sad that I fear it will never be finished no matter what we do."

The temptation to redo is the desire to go back to a sinful or dead past in order to avoid the pain of breaking free of it. Yvonne thought she was reconciling, but in reality, she was regressing. She wasn't moving forward in repentance and growth; she was trying to make something right that could never be right.

Redos aren't always acted out. Many times a redo is played out only in the mind. We get stuck on "if onlys" and keep ourselves frustrated because we know we can't rewind the tape, replay the scene, and repair it. When we try to redo our past, we end up walking the time line of our lives in a forward direction while we're facing backward. I don't know about you, but whenever I've tried to walk backward for very long, I've eventually stumbled. The only way to make things right is to move forward by facing forward—by changing and growing.

The motto for people who want to redo is, "If only I knew *then* what I know *now*." We must accept that we can apply today's wisdom only to tomorrow's temptations, not to yesterday's mistakes. Often there is no way we could have gained that wisdom if we hadn't walked our particular path. God purposed *that* we learn, and God purposed *how* we learn. We have His command to confess and repent of our wrongdoing, seek forgiveness, and make restitution. And we have His *permission to move forward,* leaving the past behind us where it belongs, free from the need to replay it over and over to try to redo the mistakes.

When we try to redo, we regress. My dictionary defines regressive behavior as a tendency to return or revert. Change never comes through regressive behavior. Interestingly, the word that immediately follows *regressive* in the dictionary is *regret.* How fitting.

THE UNDO

Trying to undo our past is much like a redo, but the motivation is different. When we try to undo our past, we aren't trying to go back and fix it—we are trying to cover it by acting as if it never happened. People usually go about this in one of two ways—attempting to undo the evidence of the sin or attempting to atone for it.

Both methods can be illustrated by abortion. Abortion itself is often motivated by the guilt and shame of sexual sin. Instead of seeing the *sin* as the problem, a desperate couple sees the *consequences* of an unwanted baby (and social embarrassment) as the problem. So they rush out to undo the evidence of their sin. Then they often will try to act as if the abortion never happened. Soon, the underlying guilt for the additional sin begins to take its toll.

When there is guilt after an abortion, it is not uncommon for the woman to become pregnant again very quickly, this time carrying the baby to term and giving birth. These babies have been called "atonement babies." They are pregnancies and babies brought about in hopes of making up for the child killed through abortion. How easily we pile one sin on top of another, trying in vain to undo what we've done!

The problems are obvious. When we attempt to undo or hide our consequences, we end up creating more of them. And *we* can't atone for our sin because only *Jesus Christ* can atone for sins. On our own, we can do nothing to undo or rectify our mistakes.

The truth is that God's grace will bring good from every situation. That will not change the past, but it will redeem it, and the good news is that *redemption is* sufficient! We can be content with it. Why? Because, as Jesus declared on the cross, "It is finished."

There is no need to undo or hide your past. Because of redemption, God is satisfied with it.

THE DON'T DO

A don't do is when we don't acknowledge loss or grief at all. There are two kinds of don't dos—denial and refusal.

Denial

Denial is a means of avoiding grief by ignoring it. For years, this was my way of dealing with grief—or rather, not dealing with it.

It took me a long time to acknowledge the loss of my first husband. I didn't deny the *sin* of our divorce, but I did deny the *loss* of him. I also denied the loss of the close relationships I had within his family. It's not that I consciously thought about what I had lost and then chose to ignore it. It's that I didn't consider what I had lost at all. I simply avoided grief by avoiding the truth. I had an underlying fear of the pain, so I essentially put my hands over my eyes. I didn't have to look at where I'd been, but having unresolved grief made it hard to see where I was going.

Refusal

Refusal is an unwillingness to call the past *the past*—the failure to recognize or acknowledge when something is over.

For example, my friend Beth's husband abandoned her and her three children. Beth remained patient and willing to reconcile for many years, but her husband steadfastly refused to return or be involved with the children. Beth did not want to be divorced, so it took her several years of life in a holding pattern before she finally faced the reality that the marriage was over.

Several more years have now gone by, and Beth remains single. But she is no longer living her life waiting for something that may never come. Only when she finally acknowledged that her husband was gone for good did she finally stop holding on and start grieving her loss so she could get on with her life.

Then there's my friend Jenni. She regretted starting a business. It wasn't making much money and required countless hours of hard work. She didn't know whether she should call the business a big mistake and let it go, or be content with the meager income and long hours. It was only after she faced and accepted the loss of her dream of short hours and big money that she was able to make a realistic decision about her business.

No matter what decisions my friends made, they had to acknowledge and accept some sort of loss. Beth accepted that her marriage was over and worked through the grief. Jenni faced her loss and decided to hold on to her business. Both were finally able to see what was true of the present and what was true of the past.

HEALING THROUGH GRIEF

If the redo, the undo, and the don't do are things to avoid while grieving, what are the proper ways to process losses?

While preparing this chapter, I reread several of my past journal entries, and I was moved to tears of compassion for the writer who expressed such heart-wrenching fear, pain, and confusion. I was also reminded how difficult grieving is—how incredibly frustrating to question heaven and hear no response and how challenging to continue to believe in God's goodness and sovereignty when all of life seems to deny it.

Much of what I wrote questioned whether the hurt would ever go away. Now that I've worked through that grief, I can testify that the pain of regret does end. It can be a slow process, for time doesn't bring about healing, and neither do we. Only God can heal, and He does so in His time and in His way. Sometimes we have no choice but to wait for Him to move. In fact, a great portion of the time we spend in grief may be spent waiting on the Lord. During that time, in the midst of our pain, we need to do three things: carefully express our emotions, diligently guard our behavior, and earnestly apply the promise and hope of His Word to our lives.

Carefully Express Emotions

It is tempting to think that if we deny emotions, they will go away, but ultimately denial simply makes them more unbearable. Emotions are real, and we need to express them. Doing so can actually facilitate the healing process. But emotions can also deceive and lead us astray. If we don't express emotions in the proper way, they are likely to rule us and draw us into more sin, more regret, and ultimately more grief.

Unmanaged emotions, or the inappropriate expression of them, can lead to destructive behavior. For example, Yvonne, my former coworker who was having the affair, would inappropriately express her sadness over the loss of her lover directly to him—and all those stirred-up feelings would drive them back together.

Practically speaking, feelings can be drawn out and expressed appropriately any number of ways:

- Talking—preferably with objective, mature believers who will tell you the truth in love.
- Journaling—writing can be both clarifying and cathartic.
- Writing letters—these do not necessarily need to be (and often shouldn't be) sent.
- Listening to music—especially songs that help express emotion while at the same time building faith.

Then there are what I believe to be the two most important ways of expressing grief appropriately: crying and praying. Crying is God's provision for cleansing emotion. Our society is not very sympathetic to that provision (especially for men), so you may struggle to give yourself permission to cry. As my friends can testify, it took me years to let myself grieve by weeping. Now I encourage people to let nothing stop them from crying. I believe that, next to prayer, crying is the key to surviving grief.

I say *next to prayer* because including God in our emotional responses is critical to our relationship with Him. Prayers of grief, however, are often when God seems most silent—most unwilling to give us the help we desire. At least that's how it seemed to me. Much of my pain was frustration and sadness born from God's refusal to take the loss away—or to answer for it in some logical way—despite my impassioned prayers for Him to do so.

Not only was I hurting; I felt that God had abandoned me. I found no comfort in the idea that God had a reason for my suffering, because He wasn't telling me what it was. At times my only solace was that God Himself knew what it was like to feel abandoned, for His Son Jesus had cried out from the cross, "My God, my God, why have you forsaken me?" (Matthew 27:46). I reasoned that if God the Father could abandon God the Son for a purpose, my loneliness might be for a purpose as well.

Sometimes it is simply best to tell God how we feel about His silence and our loss. Often we hold our feelings back because we don't want Him to know how infuriated we are or how much we doubt Him. We seem to operate under the old adage, "If you don't have anything nice to say, don't say anything at all." But that's not God's instruction. The Bible is full of men and women who fully expressed their emotions to God. As Philip Yancey points out:

> One bold message in the Book of Job is that you can say anything to God. Throw at him your grief, your anger, your doubt, your bitterness, your betrayal, your disappointment—he can absorb them all. As often as not, spiritual giants of the Bible are shown *contending* with God. They prefer to go away limping, like Jacob, rather than to shut God out. In this respect, the Bible prefigures a tenet of modern psychology: you can't really deny your feelings or make them disappear, so you might as well express them.[1]

Diligently Guard Behavior

One discovery I made while working through grief over my past was that, while we are grieving, we are extremely vulnerable to temptation and failure. To a large degree, we will behave according to how we feel, and since grief feels bad, it can lead us into temptation. If we give in to it, our bad behavior will lead to more bad feelings.

Pain can easily lead us to sin because often we want nothing more than relief. So we reach for alcohol, medication, questionable movies and television, or the arms of a lover to comfort us and numb our pain. And in the end we have more regret, more loss, more hurt.

How do we avoid this vicious cycle? The next chapter is devoted entirely to the subject of avoiding further regret. For now let's look at one foundational behavior we must avoid and some in which we must engage, especially while we're grieving.

The one thing we must not do is ignore God. When we are hurting and God seems distant, it is tempting to justify neglecting Him. After all, it feels as if He's neglecting us. What's the point of seeking Him when He refuses to answer? Philip Yancey admits:

> I know too well my own instinctive response to the hid-
> denness of God: I retaliate by ignoring him…. God can
> deal with every human response save one. He cannot abide
> the response I fall back on instinctively: an attempt to
> ignore him or treat him as though he does not exist.[2]

Ignoring God is not the answer, because He is our only hope. Only in Him do we find the strength to obey. Only in Him will healing come. If we ignore God, we set ourselves up for more failure and less healing.

The positive things we can do while we're in pain are often the most difficult. But difficult or not, they work wonders. Here they are:

- Abide in Christ. Jesus said, "Apart from me you can do nothing" (John 15:5). Take that literally. We must seek to stay close to Him even when He feels far away. Never is it more critical that we be engaged in prayer, praise, Bible study, and intimate fellowship with God and fellow believers than when we are grieving.

- Establish accountability. Often our tendency in grief is to isolate ourselves. But as we saw in chapter 6, isolation leads to desolation. Ecclesiastes 4:10 says, "Woe to the one who falls when there is not another to lift him up." A trusted friend, mentor, or pastor can mean all the difference as we persevere through pain.

Earnestly Apply Scripture

In grief our most desperate need is not relief from pain; it is application of truth. Yes, we must acknowledge the reality of our losses. Yes, we must express how we feel about those losses. But most importantly, we need to apply the truth of Scripture to our lives.

Our emotions sometimes lie, especially ones that tell us that God is uncaring, not paying attention, not good, or not in control. By constantly telling ourselves the truth—that God loves us thoroughly, knows us intimately, and has not let us go—we have hope of emerging victoriously from grief.

How desperately we want to see tangible evidence of God's sovereignty and goodness when we're in pain! During the hard time when my husband and mother were dying, God clearly showed me that He was at work. He orchestrated many situations that brought comfort, and He provided friends and family to support me. But when I began to experience deep pain as I worked through regret from my past, I saw no evidence of God's presence. I saw only my failure. I couldn't see God's goodness shining through my pain; I heard only "if only."

What I discovered is that while I believed that God was sovereign and good in the deaths of my husband and mother, my belief was based mostly on seen evidence. The pain of regret over my past, however, stretched me to finally begin to believe even what I couldn't see. For me, nothing has ever been harder.

I thought that if I could see, that if I could understand, the pain would be easier. But that's not right. Knowledge doesn't soothe hurt. The author of Lamentations knew why Israel was suffering so much. He understood completely. Yet his pain did not diminish: "My groans are many and my heart is faint" (Lamentations 1:22).

God heals us by His Holy Spirit as the Spirit illuminates the truths of God to us. He does this most often through His Word and always in accordance with it. Counselor and author Jay Adams writes:

> The Holy Spirit is a Person, not a force or a law. While he always works according to and in complete harmony with his will as he has revealed it in Scripture, he chooses his own times, means and occasions for doing his work. That is to say, the Holy Spirit works when and where and how he pleases.[3]

The Holy Spirit is the one who whispers God's goodness and sovereignty and power and love to our aching hearts. He is our comforter. But He isn't a comforter in the sense of a warm fuzzy blanket. He is, as one Bible teacher used to say to me, "A ramrod of strength up your spine." That ramrod is God's truth applied by the Holy Spirit. That truth leads to contentment.

Isn't that our goal? To be content with life? We can't change the past. All we can do is be content with how—*exactly* how—our lives have turned out. Max Lucado defines contentment as "when what we have overshadows what we want."[4] And Lindsey O'Connor defines it this way: "True contentment is being able to say, 'I am happy right here where I am'—and mean it *regardless of the circumstances*."[5] That kind of contentment comes only from believing that our loving Father truly controls this world—*your* world—and everything in it.

THE LESSONS OF LOSS

For many years I have prayed the prayer, "More of you, Lord, and less of me—no matter the cost." That prayer simultaneously inspires faith and fear in me. Faith because there is no place safer than being yielded to God; fear because I believe God sometimes answers that prayer by causing me to experience the loss of people and dreams dear to my heart. I have questioned God as to why that is. No answer yet. Perhaps loss is the only way for me to learn to cling to God and Him alone. Maybe loss is His way of teaching me that He is the only constant, sure thing. I hope I learn the lesson eventually. How liberating to rely only on the immutable, all-powerful, all-loving God instead of on changing people and circumstances! And how important, because life is full of loss.

The book of Lamentations begins with lamenting, but it ends with repentance—as it should. Understanding sin, confessing it, grieving over it, and then turning from it, are the purposes of painful consequences. Change born of faith is exactly what God is after.

When God is finished with His work, joy will overshadow the pain of loss. "The LORD is good to those whose hope is in him, to the one who seeks him; it is good to wait quietly for the salvation of the LORD" (Lamentations 3:25–26). So be strong, take heart, and wait for the Lord, for He is your only hope. In the end, because He is faithful, that hope will prove more than sufficient. In the meantime, if you are in pain, keep facing forward and keep putting one foot in front of the other.

Part Three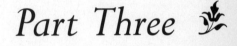

THE
TRIUMPH

12

Foresight,
Not Hindsight

How to Avoid Further Regret

❧ OBEDIENCE. It is the ultimate immunity from regret. But even though I want to obey God, I am often disobedient because of a simple, yet serious problem: It can be difficult to obey.

In order to avoid regret, we must find joy in obedience. You might be saying, "Wait a second. I'm already struggling with regret—that's why I'm reading this book. So what's the point of discussing how to *avoid* regret since it's too late for that?"

Well, if you want to put out a fire, it's best not to pour gasoline on it. It's the same with regret: One of the best ways to overcome it is to make sure you don't do any *more* things you'll regret. And let's face it: Obeying God is the only way to stop making choices that you will regret later.

One thing I've learned after talking with dozens of people who struggle with regret is this: They're often much more adept at hindsight than foresight. As they look back, they remember what they suffered when they didn't obey God and how graciously God dealt with them despite their failure. That knowledge, they think, is enough to prevent them from making poor choices in the future. I, too, am prone to this kind of thinking, but I've discovered that it is wrong.

TRIED AND UNTRUE

Gratitude for grace and awareness of the very real consequences of past failure are, of course, good things. But I have found that neither has helped me avoid failure or mistakes for very long. Let me explain.

Where Gratitude Falls Short

For Christians, gratitude should come naturally. "So then, just as you received Christ Jesus as Lord, continue to live in him, rooted and built up in him, strengthened in the faith as you were taught, and overflowing with thankfulness" (Colossians 2:6–7). Gratitude is our natural response to God's grace. When we remember all of His wonderful deeds, we cannot help but be overcome with thankfulness and awe.

But for all of the wonderful things to be said about it, gratitude doesn't provide much *strength* for obedience. Most gratitude faces backward—we're grateful for something in the past. Obedience, on the other hand, pertains to the present or future. Forcing gratitude to function as our sole strength for obedience turns grace into a loan. We end up obeying in an attempt to repay God for His past grace. Grace cannot be paid back, or else it would not be grace.

When I obey God's commands, it is rarely—if ever—without a grateful heart. Even so, I have often been both grateful and sinful at the same time. Gratitude is good, but by itself it doesn't provide enough strength to ensure obedience.

Why Awareness of Past Sins Doesn't Safeguard the Future

Remembering how badly things turned out the last time I sinned is nothing but another piece of information. Retrospective fear not only doesn't help me obey, but it also makes obedience less likely because in my pride I tend to think that "now I know better" since I've "been there, done that." But as I said in chapter 3, *knowing better* doesn't always equate to *doing better*. Knowing better will never be enough to keep me from repeating the same sin, because part of the lie of temptation is that *this time* it will be different—*this time* I'll avoid the consequences.

I don't just need to know what to do and what not to do. I don't just need to know how much pain I will endure if I do what I'm not supposed to do. What I need is an antidote for my real problem—my pride. What I need is humility.

THE INGREDIENTS OF OBEDIENCE

Gratitude for God's goodness and knowledge born of painful experience have *helped* me avoid failure and regret, but they have not been my primary source of strength for obedience. Just as faith in Christ has reconciled me to God, so strength to live obediently comes through the Holy Spirit by way of faith in God's promises. By looking forward in faith—not behind in gratitude for God's grace or in retrospective fear—I have begun to see how to obey.

Deep inside me there is a call to holiness that cannot be ignored. I long not just to be holy, but to be *happily* holy. Actually, I find myself facing temptation most often when my joy seems at odds with obedience, or, more accurately, *because* my joy seems at odds with obedience. The essence of temptation is the lie that sin will bring me more joy than obedience will. So for me, obedience is largely a fight for joy in Christ. And because there is no joy apart from faith, obedience, at its essence, is a fight for faith.

The apostle Paul asserted, "The only thing that counts is faith expressing itself through love" (Galatians 5:6). And Jesus said repeatedly, "If you love me, you will obey what I command" (John 14:15); "If anyone loves me, he will obey my teaching" (John 14:23). When I love the Lord, I obey Him. Why? Because love for God is what slays my pride, the barrier to obedience. Passionate love for God is the antidote that I need. It encompasses inexpressible and irreplaceable joy, as well as faith in all of His promises to me. Obedience flows easily out of that love. Therefore, my obedience begins when I respond to God's grace with "faith expressing itself through love."

Obedience, like salvation, comes by grace through faith. My part is to have faith, and that "comes from hearing, and hearing by the word of Christ" (Romans 10:17, NASB). Grace is God's part...and that's a done deal.

GRACE: THE DONE DEAL

I used to think that if I didn't feel the strength to obey God's commands, it must have been because I hadn't been given the grace—the ability—to obey. I thought I had to *feel* strong to *be* strong. So I'd wait to feel God's grace. And I'd continue to fail and not to feel. Talk about defeated! I was living what Rich Mullins was talking about the day I heard him on the radio. I was seeing myself as a pauper, when in reality Christ had made me a prince (well, a princess, but let's not split hairs). The fact is, the Bible teaches that once we are saved by grace we have all the grace we need to obey. Indeed, much of what we need to have faith in is the very grace by which we obey. In other words, I already have the grace to obey, but I won't take hold of that grace until I *believe* I have it. *Grace is always received by faith.*

Paul says of Christ, "The death he died, he died to sin once for all; but the life he lives, he lives to God. In the same way, count yourselves dead to sin but alive to God in Christ Jesus. Therefore, do not let sin reign in your mortal body so that you obey its evil desires" (Romans 6:10–12). What does it mean to count ourselves dead to sin but alive to God in Christ Jesus? Author Jerry Bridges paraphrases it this way: "Basically, Paul was saying...'Live out in your lives the reality of the gospel. Take advantage of and put to use all the provisions of grace God has given you in Christ.'"[1]

You are in Christ Jesus. "So you are no longer a slave, but a son; and since you are a son, God has made you also an heir" (Galatians 4:7). We are royal sons and daughters of the King, rich with every blessing and strength that the title implies. As Christians we *already have the grace to obey.* Saving grace is also sanctifying grace. Now, to become convinced of that!

Faith: Hearing Is Believing

Waiting for grace that I already had was a way of thinking that kept me defeated. I failed to see that faith is not something we do once and then stop. I believed the gospel of salvation, but I failed to believe the gospel of sanctification—the good news that, by faith, God's grace enables me to obey. Jesus set me free not only from the penalty of sin, but also from the power of sin. We *can obey* by grace through faith. As 2 Corinthians 5:17 says, "If anyone is in Christ, he is a new creation; the old has gone, the new has come!" Grace is ours. That part is a done deal.

So how do we attain faith? Jesus told us how. He said:

> "Remain in me, and I will remain in you. No branch can bear fruit by itself; it must remain in the vine. Neither can you bear fruit unless you remain in me. I am the vine; you are the branches. If a man remains in me and I in him, he will bear much fruit; apart from me you can do nothing." (John 15:4–5)

We can do nothing—especially obey God's revealed will—apart from fellowship with Christ. Jesus continued, "If you remain in me and my words remain in you, ask whatever you wish, and it will be given you. This is to my Father's glory, that you bear much fruit, showing yourselves to be my disciples" (vv. 7–8). That verse tells me that when I remain in Jesus, and His words remain in me, I can pray and have what I ask for *because my desire will be the same as His*. He changes my will to match His own. I can obey, not out of drudgery or mere duty, but out of joy because I no longer feel divided against myself.

But all of this depends on the Word. Faith comes by hearing the Word; faith comes by being in the Word. Only in Jesus do we find the faith to believe that we have the grace to obey. Only by remaining in His presence are we able to use that faith to obey.

THE BATTLE OF ABIDING

The first step, then, is to recognize that we need to abide in Him, because apart from Him we can do nothing—especially obey. As Jesus said, "Apart from me you can do nothing.… Ask whatever you wish and it will be given" (John 15:5, 7). Together, those verses echo the message of Psalm 37:4: "Delight yourself in the LORD and he will give you the desires of your heart." So the second step is to delight in the Lord, for then He will give us the desire of our heart—the strength to joyfully obey Him.

Knowing that we need to abide in Christ means that we will constantly battle the expressions of pride, such as complacency ("I know enough about God") and apathy ("I'll pay attention to God when I need Him"). In order to know God's power, we must be keenly aware of our weakness. The Holy Spirit convicts us of our inadequacy by allowing us to be overwhelmed by our flesh, our failures, and the frustrations of everyday life. But our weakness isn't the last word—God's power is.

I have witnessed great power in weakness. It appeared most vividly as I sat by the deathbeds of my husband, my mother, and, just a couple of months ago, a beloved aunt. All three of them died after battling cancer. For all three, the time came when they stopped battling and began to surrender. During those weeks, as my loved ones' bodies and minds succumbed to the process of physical death, they were in some ways more powerful than I had ever seen them. What they asked for in prayer was granted in amazing ways. And what they asked for was always important because impending death has a way of making priorities clear.

I was especially struck by the powerful work the Lord did

through my aunt in her last days. In her weakest moments, relationships that she'd prayed about, grieved over, and vigilantly tried to mend for years experienced healing. With every ear at last attentive to her words, she imparted the godly wisdom she had longed to pass on to her loved ones. Friends and family sat for hours and days by her bed, soaking up every bit of communion with her. The power of who she was, all she believed, and all that she gave was never more evident than when she was least aware of it. In the process of physical death, she became weaker and weaker as she grew ever closer to the Lord's presence. The closer she got to Him, the more powerful He became to her—and through her.

The power that flowed through my aunt on her deathbed was merely an extension of what she had experienced in life. She was a daughter of the King, and she experienced His strength because she was His child. In Him, and because of Him, she was strong.

To obey our Father, we must tap into His strength by putting our *faith* in what we know about Him. We must believe, as David did, that both God and His commandments are good.

The law of the LORD is perfect, reviving the soul. The statutes of the LORD are trustworthy, making wise the simple. The precepts of the LORD are right, giving joy to the heart. The commands of the LORD are radiant, giving light to the eyes. The fear of the LORD is pure, enduring forever. The ordinances of the LORD are sure and altogether righteous. They are more precious than gold, than much pure gold; they are sweeter than honey, than honey from the comb. By them is your servant warned; in keeping them there is great reward. (Psalm 19:7–11)

To feel as David did requires more than a quick reading of God's Word. To be filled with the truth of God, we must be engaged in deep *study* of His Word. Only then will we delight in the Lord and gain strength to joyfully obey Him. Benjamin Franklin said, "It is hard for an empty bag to stand upright." Only by feeding on the Bread of Life will we be filled and able to stand upright.

THE BEAUTY OF ABIDING

For me, the other half of abiding is *delighting* in the Lord. When we delight in Him, we enter His presence through worship. And what is worship? I love John Piper's definition: "Worship is a way of gladly reflecting back to God the radiance of His worth. This cannot be done by mere acts of duty. It can be done only when spontaneous affections arise in the heart."[2]

Worship is anything that *expresses* our desire for God, our fear and reverence of God, and our love for God. Worship includes everything that expresses our need for and devotion to God—from a broken and contrite heart such as David described in Psalm 51 to the kind of joy that made him dance before the Lord (2 Samuel 6:14). Worship isn't only a Sunday-morning event or praising God while driving down the freeway. It is also being in fellowship with other believers and serving God by joyfully serving other people. It is the outpouring of our lives to God because we are so overwhelmed by His love. That outpouring includes *obedience*. Delight in God leads to faith in God, and faith bolsters our strength to obey.

Despite my efforts to abide, I must admit that delight in God isn't always present, and when I feel that way, I know I'm in trouble—temptation is just around the corner. When our joy in knowing God diminishes, our faith shrinks, and that puts our obedience in jeopardy. Joy in abiding is the essential difference between joyful obedience under grace and dutiful obedience under law. Indeed, we are called to delight ourselves in the Lord just as clearly as we are called to obey Him.

John Piper has observed that "diminishing delight is a summons to war."[3] I agree. If we don't fight for delight in God, we will lose the battle with temptation and again have to face the truth of our weakness apart from Christ. I'm learning slowly but surely that it is far better to face that truth sooner rather than later—especially when the enemy turns up the heat.

DUKIN' IT OUT WITH DISOBEDIENCE

Chuck Swindoll said, "For unbelievers, earth is a playground where the flesh is free to romp and run wild. But for believers, earth is a battleground."[4] As long as we live on earth, we will always struggle with sin. Temptation is a call to faith in the face of doubt, to passion in the presence of indifference. Temptation to outright disobedience seems most acute when we are not expecting it and when our delight in God is diminished.

THE BLIND SIDE

Temptation usually rears its ugly head when I don't believe that God or His commands are good—or good for me. Sometimes I am blind to my unbelief and temptation takes me by surprise. I'm slowly learning what Paul meant when he said, "So, if you think you are standing firm, be careful that you don't fall!" (1 Corinthians 10:12).

It is usually when I am in pain or have a sense of need that I'm vulnerable. When I was feeling deep pain because of my failure and regret, I doubted God's sovereignty and goodness. Because I found no comfort in my faith, I was tempted to comfort myself. That is one of Satan's best strategies. He knows where we doubt God, and he aims for our blind side. He exploits every opportunity to combine what we think we *need* with what we think we *believe*. But need never justifies sin. Jesus needed food in the desert, yet He resisted Satan's temptation. The Lord not only quoted the Word, He believed it, and the devil left him. Likewise, in our times of temptation, what we need most is faith in the Word.

That's why our blind side is often our blind faith. It is difficult to believe the promises of God when we don't know or remember what they are. It is difficult to trust in a God we do not really know. If we aren't abiding in Christ, then we won't be prepared for unexpected temptation by having truth readily in mind—and we will fall. Too often we wait for temptation to come before we seek the Lord's help. We often don't realize that resisting temptation begins in the absence of temptation. It begins with abiding. Ralph Waldo Emerson could have been talking about abiding when he said, "One of the illusions of life is that the present hour is not the critical, decisive hour."

The Grace Trap

The other time I feel most tempted to sin is when the Word seems dry, fellowship seems shallow, and prayers seem to hit the ceiling. When I feel indifferent about abiding, I'm usually not far from falling into sin by way of the grace trap. The grace trap is anything that remotely sounds like this: "Well, God will forgive me, so why not?"

When we are tempted in that way, gratitude and retrospective fear *are* helpful. We need gratitude for past grace to propel us to faith in future grace, and we need retrospective fear to remind us not only of the consequences we suffered the last time we sinned, but also of the pain of repentance.

The grace trap promises easy forgiveness for sin. Retrospective fear can remind us that nothing about forgiveness is easy. Repentance is *hard*. It includes contrition and the wish that we had never sinned. Charles Spurgeon said, "Christians can never sin cheaply."[5] That's because returning to the Lord, and to His grace, requires that we pay the price of repentance and bear the consequences of sin.

We need a way out of our temptation, and we need to be shielded from the grace trap. The way out and the shield are the same—faith. Ephesians 6:16 says that with the shield of faith we "can extinguish all the flaming arrows of the evil one." When the grace trap tempts us, we need to know that we can either choose to sin and then receive forgiveness by grace through faith, or obey and receive increased joy and blessing by grace through faith.

Presented in black and white on a printed page, the choice seems obvious. But everyday life is rarely so clear and straightforward. Faith seems effortless when we feel satisfied in our relationship with the Lord. But when our joy and love for the Lord are weak, faith seems laborious. Remember what Paul said: "The only thing that counts is faith expressing itself through love" (Galatians 5:6). So when our faith is in jeopardy, what we need most is to recapture the passionate and satisfying love for God that leads to deep joy and strong faith.

"Faith stands or falls on the truth that the future with God is more satisfying than the one promised by sin," writes John Piper.[6] How do we become convinced of that truth when we feel as if we're in a spiritual drought? For me, the answer has been to examine the object of my love. I have often been surprised to find that it hasn't been God. At times, my passion wasn't for God Himself, but for the blessings He gave. When the blessings weren't apparent, neither was my passion. Other times, my passion wasn't focused on the magnificence of God's glory, but on the glory He was working in *me*. The object of my love became the gift instead of the Giver. I became focused on all that God was doing for me and in me instead of being focused on God Himself. When I did so, the object of my passion ultimately became *I* instead of the great *I AM*.

Passionate love for God, on the other hand, is always in response to His love for me. When I focus on Him and His magnificent love for me, I cannot help responding with passionate love for Him. And where there is passionate love, there is no grace trap.

Philip Yancey addresses what he calls this "loophole" of grace this way:

Would a groom on his wedding night hold the following conversation with his bride? "Honey, I love you so much, and I'm eager to spend my life with you. But I need to work out a few details. After we're married, how far can I go with other women? Can I sleep with them? Kiss them? You don't mind a few affairs now and then, do you? I know it might hurt you, but just think of all the opportunities you'll have to forgive me after I betray you!"[7]

That's the foolishness of the grace trap. Passionate love for God nullifies the possibility of viewing grace in such an absurd way. And passionate love *for* God is our natural response when our focus is really *on* God.

FINDING GOD'S WILL: EENY, MEENY, MINEY, MO?

Failure and regret don't always come as a result of outright sin. They often come in the wake of a missed opportunity, a failure to choose the best path at a fork in the road of life, or even a poor decision about time priorities. The people who experience regret over such things are often those who are searching for God's particular will. They feel regret because they fear they didn't find it.

The Bible is clear that God has no trouble communicating His desires to us. Psalm 32:8 promises, "I will instruct you and teach you in the way you should go; I will counsel you and watch over you." From Adam to Abraham to Peter to Paul, God has shown that He can and does direct us. So what's the hassle about? Why the struggle to know which way to go? Why do we often feel as if we had better guidance than to play "eeny, meeny, miney, mo"?

J. I. Packer states part of the problem:

Earnest Christians seeking guidance often go wrong about it. Why is this? Often the reason is that they have a distorted notion of the nature and method of divine guidance. They look for a will-o'-the-wisp, overlooking the guidance that is ready to hand and laying themselves open to all sorts of delusions. Their basic mistake is to think of guidance as essentially *inward prompting by the Holy Spirit, apart from the written Word.*[8]

I remember a Bible teacher once telling me, "Do not be so foolish as to test God. Do not look for God's will by saying, 'Oh, Lord, if You want me to go to such and such college then please make a chicken run across my television screen. But if You want the other college, make a goat run across the screen.'" While she was being facetious, she made a good point. It's easy to want concrete guidance from the Lord about day-to-day decisions that the Bible does not address.

Probably the best instruction I've ever received on knowing the will of God came from John MacArthur, who said essentially this: When you are abiding in Christ and diligently seeking to follow Him, you don't have to search for God's will because you *are* in His will. In other words, if you're following God's *already* revealed will to be "saved, Spirit-filled, sanctified, submissive, and suffering," then God's particular will for you is *whatever you want.*[9] Why? Because when you are saved and abiding in Christ and living a life that seeks God in every way, He is the one who determines your desires. Your job is to be in the "already revealed" will of God and then to passionately pursue whatever He places on your heart.

Of course, sometimes when we follow God's revealed will, we have equally strong desires that seem to conflict. And everyday life doesn't always give us the luxury of sitting quietly and waiting for a clear answer. We often have to wait even while we're on the move. As John MacArthur puts it, "Knowing God's will may mean pushing down a narrow line until you hit a dead end. At that point, God will open a door so wide, you won't be able to see around it—only through it!"[10]

Waiting and moving…it's like jogging in place at a crosswalk and watching for the green light.

IT'S HOW YOU PLAY THE GAME

I would love to say that I'll never again struggle with regret brought on by bad decisions. But I don't know that. I don't know what lies ahead or what choices I will make in the future. I do know, of course, that I still wrestle with temptation and sin. I know that I will never "arrive" this side of heaven. I'm trying hard not to forget that and not to place unrealistic expectations on myself—just as I am learning not to place them on others. But I also know that, having failed terribly in my life and then lived with the worldly sorrow of regret, I am determined to continue the struggle to obey, even when it hurts.

I would much rather fight against my pride, and for the delights of faith in Christ, than fight the battle of repentance and grief. I would much rather have Jesus instruct me and humble me than have my own failure break my heart. I would much rather live in the foresight of faith than the hindsight of sin.

That's what I'd prefer, but there are no guarantees. As Solomon taught in Ecclesiastes, there is no formula to ensure happiness, holiness, and success in life. We can only set our eyes on the right pursuit. So we fear God and pursue righteousness because the joys of wisdom are deeper than the joys of folly. We enjoy all life has to offer in that pursuit; we don't beat ourselves up for failing; we accept God's grace; and we move on down the road, knowing that one day we'll understand the reasons everything happened. That's faith. And that's really the only thing we have.

My intention in this chapter has not been to present a formula for obedience, but to show that it is possible to obey and avoid regret. It's possible only by grace through faith in the Lord Jesus Christ. God's revealed will is that we fight the fight of faith. When we temporarily lose that fight, we put our hope in God's sovereignty, knowing that in both failure and obedience, He is conforming us to the image of His Son.

This chapter began with one word: *obedience*. It will end with another word. You cannot separate the two. If you find the strength to obey, it will be because God's grace has empowered you through joy, love, and—most of all—*faith*.

13

Good-bye...Hello

Moving from Heartache to Hope

🌿 I KNEW I had triumphed over regret when I believed that my failures had conformed me further to the image of Jesus and when I was content with how God was choosing to bring that transformation about. I came to understand—and truly believe—the words in Romans 11:36: "For from him and through him and to him are all things. To him be the glory forever."

It's difficult, if not impossible, to say "if only" while believing the truth that *all* things are *from*, *through*, and *to* the Lord. Indescribable peace comes with believing that all the circumstances of our lives are from the Lord's hand and that they are always under His control. That includes the family we were born into, the time in history we were born, our unique personalities, every success and healing, and every failure, pain, and regret. Peace reaches its fullness with the belief that everything, good and bad, exists to bring glory to God. Evil glorifies God by being in contrast to Him, while holiness glorifies God by being in harmony with Him. All of it exists for the Lord's glory and purposes.

FROM TRAGEDY TO TRIUMPH

It has been five years since my husband and mother died from cancer—and five years since the depth of my regret finally hit me. I spent my first two years as a single mother grieving the loss of my husband, the loss of my mother, and the loss of my dreams. But during that time—in the middle of my grief—I sought the Lord and asked Him for healing. It was a difficult two years, full of ups and downs. One moment I despaired, the next I hoped. One day I triumphed in faith, the next day I merely coped. One week I felt young, the next like life had passed me by.

But as I continued to seek the truth, slowly at first, and then with increasing momentum, the light began to overcome the darkness in me. God's Word rescued me from all the guilt, secrecy, anger, unforgivingness, misconceptions about God, and failure to grieve that had plagued me for so long. His Word took me from tragedy to triumph. He gave me the peace that eclipses pain.

You can have that same peace. God's truth can enable you to overcome regret, get past your past, and move forward with renewed peace, confidence, and hope.

Deal with the Guilt

The first step in releasing regret is to receive God's forgiveness. To do this, we must first understand sin, conviction, and repentance, and then resist the pride and blame that keep us from true repentance. Sometimes it isn't our sin we're sorry for, but the consequences of it. There is a sorrow, however, that leads to repentance, and it's the only useful kind of regret (see 2 Corinthians 7:9–10). This regret reveals the debris of our broken lives and helps us appreciate the redemption offered by Christ through His *finished* work on the Cross.

Surrender Your Secrets

Secrecy places us in an emotional and spiritual prison. When we try to hide sin from God and don't live authentically before others, we are isolated and bound, like prisoners. Hidden regret cannot be healed, and untold grief leads to unspeakable pain. Through confession we find restoration, healing, and greater spiritual maturity as we yield ourselves to God. We must be wise in how, when, and to whom we confess, but when we do, we gain freedom from the confining prison cell. Paradoxically, we must surrender in order to be free.

Turn Anger into Forgiveness

When we don't forgive, we inevitably end up bitter and blaming— and, consequently, focused on the past. To dispel regret we must choose to forgive—to bear scars of sacrifice instead of scars of cynicism. We may not ever be able to totally forget the past, but it will become less vivid after we forgive. Indeed, we *must* forgive or we will not be *able* to forget. Forgiveness and forgetfulness are inextricably connected.

Correct Your Misconceptions about God

Diving deeply into God's Word for pearls of truth can be daunting, but the reward makes it worthwhile. To do away with paralyzing regret, we must endeavor to know God. When we have ideas about God that aren't based on truth, we have faux pearls—and faux pearls lead to faux pas because what we believe about God directly affects our thoughts, emotions, and actions. Therefore, our understanding of God and how He operates in our lives matters tremendously. Our choice is to live according to truth or suffer consequences. Specifically, we must be convinced at the core of our being that God is sovereign and good—and that He always wants what's best for us.

Grieve Your Loss

Good-bye is one of the hardest words to say, but doing so begins the process of accepting what we've lost because of choices we regret. Because of them, we've lost not only tangible things, but also parts of our dreams. The only way to say good-bye to a dream is to know and *believe* that God is eager to give us new ones. Grief will come, but it will not overwhelm us if we know God. When we accept our losses, we can begin to dream anew. This will give us hope, purpose, and focus—on the future.

Are you focused on the future because you have made regret a thing of the past? Have you come to believe that God is working in *all* things to conform you to the image of Jesus? Have you learned to be content with how He is choosing to bring about that transformation? If so, you are moving from heartache to hope, from tragedy to triumph.

Sometimes, however, overcoming the regret born from failure isn't our only need. Sometimes we must also address the useless methods of dealing with our pain that keep us in a cycle of regret.

FROM MILLSTONE TO MILESTONE

Jesus said that He came into the world "that they may have life, and have it to the full" (John 10:10). A life marked by regret is not *full*. It is a life of coping, agonizing, struggling to break free. Often we try to cope with the pain of regret by seeking comfort in unhealthy ways, such as excessive use of alcohol, overeating, gambling, or promiscuity. These pursuits only make us more miserable and bring more regret. We cope to avoid regret, and then we regret our methods of coping. It is indeed a vicious cycle. Fortunately there is one thing that can break this cycle—truth.

When we begin to apply God's truth to our guilt, we don't need to find ways to cope with our regret. Sins that cause more regret become less appealing, and the cycle stops. As we learn to abide in Him, aligning our wills with His, we apply the truth that corrects our shortsighted, self-centered vision, and our desire and ability to avoid destructive behavior increase. Millstones that once hung around our neck fall away, and we begin reaching milestones on the journey toward wholeness. Appropriating the power and strength of God's truth begins the process of getting past our past.

Christians should never be content merely to *cope* with life. The Christian life is a radical life of passionate service. That may sometimes seem like a scary thing, but it's part of the joyous, abundant life that Jesus promised us. Some time ago on an airplane, I overheard the man in front of me telling the woman next to him about all the risky and adventurous things he was pursuing. He finished by saying, "Well, I've always heard that if you're not living on the edge, you're taking up too much space." I chuckled when I heard that, but I suppose that's true. Christians, of all people, should desire to live on the edge—fervently serving God and going all-out in our quest to grow in Him.

We have a responsibility as Christians to get and stay healthy—spiritually, emotionally, and, as much as it's up to us, physically. People all around us are dying. Who will help them if the ones most capable of offering assistance are too preoccupied with nursing their wounds? If we seek an abundant life, a defeatist attitude is not an option. What we need is an attitude of confidence and trust in the Lord—faith that God can, will, and does have a joyous plan for our lives and that no circumstance will keep us from it. It all comes down to what we believe. It *always* comes down to what we believe.

What I believe is that the abundant life I now live is partly because of my mistakes in the past. For instance, were it not for my past choices, I wouldn't have the children I now have. How can I regret them? And were it not for my regret, I wouldn't be writing to you. I'm certainly grateful for that. Life is always a mixed bag of blessings and hardships. One goes with the other—always. I'm learning to see the whole picture of my life instead of just looking at the snapshots of my past or the mental picture of what I thought my life was supposed to be.

I had drawn that mental picture with lines that were bold and sure, and when God began redrawing it, in my frustration, I at first refused to see the beauty of His work. But over and over, the Master Artist has surprised me with a portrait of a life that I never could have imagined—and over and over that surprise has been my joy.

FROM PILLAR TO SHAKER

I said earlier that we should not make choices based solely on our feelings. Our emotions deceive us when they tell us that we need comfort more than we need Christ, or that we've messed up our lives beyond repair and destroyed our purpose. Those emotions must not guide our behavior.

But when your emotions line up with the Word of God, *live them to the fullest*. When your emotions tell you that in God's eyes you are no different from any other forgiven sinner, they tell you the truth. When they tell you that you are free from the penalty and power of sin and that your purpose on earth is not fulfilled until the Lord calls you home, they are right. When they tell you that faith in God that is expressed by loving Him and other people is all that matters, they do not deceive you. And when you know the truth, and your emotions express the truth, you are ready to passionately pursue whatever forward-facing purpose God lays on your heart.

When we face the future enthusiastically, knowing that God is directing our path, we are transformed from a pillar of salt to a shaker of salt, able to season a bland world with love, grace, and truth. And when we do that, we reflect the glory of God.

We first reflect God's beauty with our *being,* not our *doing.* Our doing *stems from* our being. When we are what He created us to be, we will do what He created us to do. He is magnified in the *process* of our healing, and He is magnified in the *product* of our healing.

So when healing comes, get going. Serve God however you are gifted, wherever you are. Have a dream and pursue it passionately. Don't be surprised if God uses your past failures and regrets to serve a dying world and a hurting church. My brother-in-law, Larry, after spending years addicted to drugs, recently graduated summa cum laude from seminary. He now has a unique ministry to youth and the hurting. Trust God, and He will give you purpose, strength, and perseverance to accomplish all that He has joyfully prepared for you to do. Psalm 126:5–6 proclaims, "Those who sow in tears will reap with songs of joy. He who goes out weeping, carrying seed to sow, will return with songs of joy, carrying sheaves with him."

On many occasions, I have been asked the reason for my hope. You may be asked the same thing. The questions come in different forms: How can you be content after all you've been through? Why are you so happy? How can you be joyful in the middle of your suffering?

The apostle Peter said, "Always be prepared to give an answer to everyone who asks you to give the reason for the hope that you have" (Peter 3:15). My answer? Failure is hard, but God is good. And life isn't out of control; it's just out of *my* control. I've learned that no matter what—success or failure, gain or loss—God is good and He is sovereign. All the time. Those truths not only got me past my past, but they have also given me a constant joy and deep satisfaction with life. They can do the same for you.

Recommended Reading

Jonathan Edwards, *Freedom of the Will* (Morgan, Pa.: Soli Deo Gloria Publications, 1996)

Martin Luther, *The Bondage of the Will* (Grand Rapids, Mich.: Fleming H. Revell, 1957)

A. W. Pink, *The Sovereignty of God* (Grand Rapids, Mich.: Baker Book House, 1930)

John Piper, *Desiring God* (Sisters, Ore.: Multnomah Publishers, 1996)

R. C. Sproul, *Willing to Believe* (Grand Rapids, Mich.: Baker Books, 1997)

Notes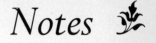

CHAPTER ONE

1. Charles Haddon Spurgeon, *The Cheque-Book of the Bank of Faith* (Pasadena, Calif.: Pilgrim Publications, 1975), vi.
2. Frederick Buechner, *Wishful Thinking* (San Francisco: Harper & Row, 1973), 96.

CHAPTER THREE

1. R. C. Sproul quotes this story in *Willing to Believe* (Grand Rapids, Mich.: Baker Books, 1997), 109.

CHAPTER FOUR

1. John F. MacArthur Jr., *The Freedom and Power of Forgiveness* (Wheaton, Ill.: Crossway Books, 1998), 7.
2. A. W. Pink, *The Attributes of God* (Grand Rapids, Mich.: Baker Book House, 1975), 38–9.
3. C. S. Lewis, *A Grief Observed* (San Francisco: HarperSanFrancisco, 1961), 76.
4. R. C. Sproul, *Willing to Believe* (Grand Rapids, Mich.: Baker Books, 1997), 54.
5. Max Lucado, *God Came Near* (Portland, Ore.: Multnomah Publishers, 1986), 23.
6. J. I. Packer, *Knowing God* (Downers Grove, Ill.: InterVarsity Press, 1973), 46–7.

7. Max Lucado, *No Wonder They Call Him the Savior* (Portland, Ore.: Multnomah Publishers, 1986), 56.

CHAPTER FIVE

1. Charles Spurgeon quoted in *Devotional Classics,* ed. Richard J. Foster and James Bryan Smith, (San Francisco: HarperSanFrancisco, 1993), 334.
2. Ibid.
3. Max Lucado, *No Wonder They Call Him the Savior* (Portland, Ore.: Multnomah Publishers, 1986), 56.
4. James C. Dobson, *Love Must Be Tough* (Waco, Tex.: Word Books, 1983), 80.

CHAPTER SIX

1. Dr. Henry Cloud and Dr. John Townsend, *Boundaries* (Grand Rapids, Mich.: Zondervan, 1992), 217.
2. St. Augustine, *Confessions* (New York: Penguin, 1961), 207.
3. Tim and Beverly LaHaye, *The Act of Marriage* (Grand Rapids, Mich.: Zondervan, 1976), 255.
4. H. Norman Wright, *Questions Women Ask in Private* (Ventura, Calif.: Regal Books, 1993), 192–3.
5. John F. MacArthur Jr., *The Freedom and Power of Forgiveness* (Wheaton, Ill.: Crossway Books, 1998), 185.
6. From a conversation with Dr. Russ Massey, M.B.A., M.A., L.P.C.

CHAPTER SEVEN

1. John F. MacArthur Jr., *The Freedom and Power of Forgiveness* (Wheaton, Ill.: Crossway Books, 1998), 161.

2. C. S. Lewis, *Mere Christianity* (New York: Macmillan, 1952), 105–6.

3. Philip Yancey, *What's So Amazing About Grace?* (Grand Rapids, Mich.: Zondervan, 1997), 93.

4. MacArthur, *The Freedom and Power of Forgiveness,* 112.

5. Ibid., 166.

6. Charles R. Swindoll, *Hope Again* (Dallas, Tex.: Word, 1996), 94.

7. Yancey, *What's So Amazing About Grace?* 206.

8. Charlotte Bronte, *Jane Eyre* (New York: Miramax Book/Hyperion, 1996), v–vi.

9. Yancey, *What's So Amazing About Grace?* 11.

10. Neil T. Anderson, *The Bondage Breaker* (Eugene, Ore.: Harvest House, 1990), 195.

CHAPTER EIGHT

1. J. I. Packer, *Knowing God* (Downers Grove, Ill.: InterVarsity Press, 1973), 29.

2. A. W. Tozer, *The Knowledge of the Holy* (Lincoln, Nebr.: Back to the Bible, 1961), 8.

3. Quote taken from the Web site Great Books Online—Bartlett's Quotations: http://www.bartleby.com/99/439.html.

4. Philip Yancey, *The Jesus I Never Knew* (Grand Rapids, Mich.: Zondervan, 1995), 117.

5. Packer, *Knowing God,* 32.

6. Martin Luther, *The Bondage of the Will* (Grand Rapids, Mich.: Revell, 1957), 55–6.

7. Packer, *Knowing God,* 196.

8. John Piper, *Desiring God* (Sisters, Ore.: Multnomah Publishers, 1996), 35.

9. R. C. Sproul, *Willing to Believe* (Grand Rapids, Mich.: Baker Books, 1997), 91.

10. Luther, *The Bondage of the Will,* 80–1.

11. To study the theological debate over God's sovereignty versus man's free will, see the recommended reading in the appendix.

12. Sproul, *Willing to Believe,* 28–9.

13. Ibid., 27.

14. Piper, *Desiring God,* 42.

CHAPTER NINE

1. A. W. Pink, *The Sovereignty of God* (Edinburgh: Banner of Truth Trust, 1976), 149.

2. Ibid., 146.

3. Larry Crabb, *Finding God* (Grand Rapids, Mich.: Zondervan, 1993), 11.

4. Ruth Myers, *31 Days of Praise* (Sisters, Ore.: Multnomah Publishers, 1994), 60–1.

5. Pink, *The Sovereignty of God,* 43–4.

6. Chris Fabry, *The 77 Habits of Highly Ineffective Christians* (Downers Grove, Ill.: InterVarsity Press, 1997), 51.

7. Ibid., 29–30.

8. Ben Carson, M.D., with Cecil Murphey, *Think Big* (Grand Rapids, Mich.: Zondervan, 1992), 174.

CHAPTER TEN

1. Extracts from Tinh's story, "Desperate Dash to Freedom," are taken from W. Stanley Mooneyham, *Sea of Heartbreak* (Plainfield, N.J.: Logos International; Minneapolis, Minn.: Jeremy Books, 1980), 39–47.
2. Philip Yancey, *Disappointment with God* (Grand Rapids, Mich.: Zondervan, 1988), 240.
3. Ibid., 201.

CHAPTER ELEVEN

1. Philip Yancey, *Disappointment with God* (Grand Rapids, Mich.: Zondervan, 1988), 235.
2. Ibid., 234–5.
3. Jay Adams, *Competent to Counsel* (Nutley, N.J.: Presbyterian and Reformed Publishing Co., 1970), 22.
4. Max Lucado, *No Wonder They Call Him the Savior* (Portland, Ore.: Multnomah Publishers, 1986), 60.
5. Lindsey O'Connor, *If Mama Ain't Happy, Ain't Nobody Happy* (Eugene, Ore.: Harvest House, 1996), 79.

CHAPTER TWELVE

1. Jerry Bridges, *The Discipline of Grace* (Colorado Springs: NavPress, 1994), 74.
2. John Piper, *Desiring God* (Sisters, Ore.: Multnomah Publishers, 1996), 83.
3. John Piper, *Future Grace* (Sisters, Ore.: Multnomah Publishers, 1995), 316.

4. Charles R. Swindoll, *Hope Again* (Dallas, Tex.: Word, 1996), 73.

5. Charles Spurgeon, *Morning and Evening* (New Kensington, Pa.: Whitaker House, 1997), 305.

6. Piper, *Future Grace,* 326.

7. Philip Yancey, *What's So Amazing About Grace?* (Grand Rapids, Mich.: Zondervan, 1997), 180–90.

8. J. I. Packer, *Knowing God* (Downers Grove, Ill.: InterVarsity Press, 1973), 212.

9. John F. MacArthur Jr., *Found: God's Will* (Colorado Springs: Chariot Victor, 1977), 54.

10. Ibid., 59.